Improving Teaching and Learning

What's Your Relationship Quotient?

Rebecca Wilke

ScarecrowEducation
Lanham, Maryland • Toronto • Oxford
2005

Published in the United States of America
by ScarecrowEducation
An imprint of The Rowman & Littlefield Publishing Group, Inc.
4501 Forbes Boulevard, Suite 200, Lanham, Maryland 20706
www.scarecroweducation.com

PO Box 317
Oxford
OX2 9RU, UK

British Library Cataloguing in Publication Information Available

Library of Congress Cataloging-in-Publication Data

Wilke, Rebecca Lynn.
  Improving teaching and learning : what's your relationship quotient? /
Rebecca Lynn Wilke.
    p. cm.
  Includes bibliographical references and index.
  ISBN 1-57886-195-0 (pbk. : alk. paper)
  1. Teacher-student relationships. 2. Teachers—Professional relationships.
I. Title.
LB1033.W463 2005
371.102—dc22   2004025257

∞™ The paper used in this publication meets the minimum requirements of
American National Standard for Information Sciences—Permanence of
Paper for Printed Library Materials, ANSI/NISO Z39.48-1992.
Manufactured in the United States of America.

After a lifetime of experiencing wonderful relationships, the task of deciding where to even start this dedication as well as whom to offer my thankfulness for the acceptance, support, and encouragement I've received over the years seems daunting. Yet I feel I truly must begin at the beginning. . . . To my parents, who not only brought me into this world but also taught me from my earliest days what it meant to love and be loved. I wish many blessings upon all of my teachers and mentors along life's journey—they gave me my first glimpses at how important connecting with kids actually is to educating young hearts and minds. Finally, I am grateful to God, who reveals to me each day what real "relationship" is all about.

One hundred years from now, it will not matter what kind of car you drove, what kind of house you lived in, how much you had in your bank account nor what your clothes looked like, but the world may be a better place because you were important in the life of a child.

—Anonymous

Contents

Preface

If you asked the average person to sum up the purpose of education in a few sentences, the three Rs would more than likely be included somewhere in the definition. These simple descriptors from days gone by— reading, 'riting, and 'rithmetic—meant that the next generation would learn the essential tools to get by in life. Early in America's history, people realized that educating children would improve society and ensure the security of our nation.

This basic curriculum expanded as the nation itself grew, and the three Rs became the backbone for our assessment of intelligence. Yet an equally important, though less visible, R also existed and evolved during the development of our educational system: the *relationship* between teacher and student. For centuries, this relationship quotient has supported the implementation of content, the interactions inside and outside of the classroom, and the intricate and dynamic community that exists on every school campus.

At the dawn of the twenty-first century, all educators must become more cognizant of how every relationship profoundly affects the world. Innumerable problems can arise when kids are lonely and disconnected. The use of drugs, involvement in gangs, acts of violence, and attempts at suicide are just a few of the frantic ways our young people are crying out for attention. If these dilemmas are not dealt with inside our homes and schools, they will multiply and manifest themselves throughout society. Although knowledge, instruction, and learning are essential to educating young minds, understanding how a person relates to and can interact with others more effectively may be one of the most vital aspects of education we can pass on to future generations. This relationship quotient—RQ, if you will—may even be more essential to success than one's intellectual quotient.

Can studying RQ have as dramatic an impact on students and school communities as class-size reduction or increased accountability? The answer is yes—most definitely yes! That's what *Improving Teaching and Learning: What's Your Relationship Quotient?* is all about. By discovering more about the dynamics of basic relationship formation, educators can take a closer look at how to improve the lives of their students as well as the environment in which they work day to day. This book will give teachers new ideas on how to improve the connections within their own classrooms so more time can be spent on the actual learning process. Understanding the steps that lead toward building better relationships will be like finding the missing piece to the educational puzzle! By cultivating vital interpersonal interactions, everyone involved in schools—from students to staff to parents—will feel more empowered and excited about what the future holds.

After twenty years of working in classrooms and corporations, I can assure you that relationships are at the core of satisfaction and success in our professional as well as our personal lives. Although many people may be aware of the importance of such connections, most of us have not been supplied with the tools and techniques to formulate optimal relationships with the individuals with whom we interact on a daily basis. This book is designed to assist educators in this simple yet strategic process. Not only will you see immediate results with your students as they improve communication, cultivate cultural understanding, and begin connecting within the diverse community in which they live, but you will also discover that you're moving closer to your dream of becoming an exceptional educator.

Note: Many of the names in this book have been changed. If you recognize your story, please accept my deep appreciation for being part of my journey in education—and in life!

CHAPTER 1

Relationships Are the Center of the Universe

After a long first week of school, I noticed that Jason still hovered at the classroom door, even though all of my other students had left for the day. He seemed uneasy, yet he obviously had something on his mind. I set the papers that I had been organizing down on my desk and walked over to him.

Jason stood out in this particular group of sixth graders for several reasons. First, he weighed at least fifty pounds more than the next largest child in the class. Second, the black T-shirt he wore each day represented a then-popular heavy metal group. Third, despite his long blond Shirley Temple–like curls, he had a "tough guy" attitude about him—as if he had already experienced half a lifetime in his twelve short years on earth.

But standing in the doorway that afternoon, he looked almost shy.

"Jason, can I help you?" I asked.

"Well, not really . . ." he stammered, shuffling his feet a bit. "I just wanted to tell you something."

"Oh, then I'm so glad you stayed behind," I replied. "What is it?"

"I just wanted to let you know that I'm going to be good for you this year. I'm not going to do things to you that I did to my teacher last year."

I swallowed before I ventured to ask the question that immediately popped into my mind. Trying to sound calm, I finally spoke, "Oh—and what kinds of things did you do?"

Jason quickly retorted, "Not too nice of things, Mrs. Wilke. But I promise I won't throw any chairs at you!"

With that, Jason flashed me an impish grin and lumbered out the door. I stood frozen for a few minutes. Should I be relieved? Other terrible images of "not too nice of things" flashed before me, but so too did the memory of Jason's timid stance in the doorway and the soft sound in his voice as he made me a solemn promise to be good this year.

What had made the difference in this boy's desire to please rather than punish his teacher—and after only one week of school had passed? The answer that came to me then—and it's one that I am more certain of after twenty-plus years of teaching—is that the positive relationship that I was determined to establish with my students had made an immediate impact in Jason's life. I believe he could sense that I truly cared for each of the kids in my class—and that included him. Maybe it was the first time he'd felt that way. But looking into his eyes that day, I could see that I'd made a connection at a very personal level—and that was all that mattered.

I wish I could tell you that year with Jason was perfect, but you probably figured out that we would face some problems. He did have a few struggles with his temper—directed at his fellow students and even, at times, at me. But he never threw a chair. In fact, he never threw anything. And most of those minor outbursts were resolved fairly quickly when I was able to intervene and help him think through the situation.

As the years have passed and I've taken my teaching skills to the university and corporate settings, I am more resolved than ever that the formation of positive relationships is an integral component to personal and professional success. Indeed, as my husband, Dr. Steve Wilke, often shares with executives, *relationships are the center of the universe, and without them nothing we do really matters.*

Think about that concept for a moment. What would life be like without other people? Why would you want to get up in the morning if you had no one to communicate with, no one to share your life experiences with, and no one to interact with even on the most basic levels? Would you even want to earn money that didn't in some way benefit someone else? What would every day, every month, and every year be like if you had only your computer, television, and car radio to keep you company?

Visions of Ray Bradbury's futuristic tales come to mind when I contemplate these kinds of questions. Life in that kind of world would be cold, emotionally empty, and totally unsatisfying.

Yet how much time do we devote to understanding and improving the relationships in our day-to-day lives? The answer for most of us would probably be little to none, and often there are very sound reasons for this. Life is extremely busy. There is so much that we need to accomplish on an average day that finding time to fit in one more project—even one that we know would benefit us as well as everyone around us—is difficult. The very thought of sparing an hour of our already packed schedules to reflect on how we interact with our fellow human beings may be overwhelming.

But let's get back to the key issue. If relationships are at the center of your universe, shouldn't you be spending more time contemplating how they can function better? This includes not only how they work, but also how you can take steps to keep all of them operating at an optimum level.

What if I told you that spending time honing the skills necessary to enhance your "relationship quotient" with others would dramatically improve your teaching? How about if I convinced you that discipline problems decrease in classrooms where positive connections between teachers and students exist? Would you have more incentive to investigate how *the art of relating* might really aid you—and your students—in the educational experience?

Like Jason did for me that day, I too can make you a definite promise. *Investing quality time now on this essential aspect of your professional life will be like finding the missing piece of a puzzle: suddenly, everything will seem to fall into place!* The other three Rs that you've been teaching will make more sense as the students connect with you, their teacher, on a personal level. Yes, you will still have struggles, but these too will be less difficult, because you will have learned to enlist the help of fellow teachers, administrators, and parents. You'll also be able to catch a glimpse of the bigger picture in education: helping students learn how to relate to one another truly prepares them to become members of the global world that is their future. As we strive together to build great relationships in today's diverse classrooms and schools, we may finally be able to reach our goal of educational excellence in this nation.

DISCONNECTED KIDS CAN'T LEARN

As you begin to picture the world from the perspective of relationships, you will start to see just how important interactions with others are in your professional and personal lives. School campuses are an excellent example of the importance of relationships. Standing on the curb in front of any elementary, middle, or high school will awaken the observer's eye to what the French word *relater*, "to connect," really means. Kids scurry from cars or are escorted by parents. Some walk hand in hand with siblings. Others skip with friends to the playground. Boys hang with boys. Girls chat with girls. Boyfriends and girlfriends smile and giggle. Teachers wave hello. Administrators answer questions. People of all ages, shapes, sizes, backgrounds, cultures, and languages are in action—everywhere!

These person-to-person connections are evident all over campus, all day long. Whether in classrooms or courtyards, in libraries or lunchrooms, on basketball courts or in bathrooms—students, teachers, support staff, volunteers, visitors, and parents spend the majority of the school day interacting with one another. In other words, *our educational institutions are really mere snapshots of the real world: they are places where people work at the art of relating.*

These interactions are not only essential for the learning process to occur, but they are also considered to be a major purpose of education in general. Indeed, "socialization" has been one of the underlying goals of schooling since the early days of American history (Spring, 2002). Many educational experts believe that helping students learn how to relate to others should be a goal of education so that young people are prepared to become functioning members of society (Jensen & Kiley, 2000). This also coincides with current reform efforts to promote values and morals within caring communities, both at school and in the world in general (DeRoche & Williams, 2001; Jensen & Kiley, 2000).

Today's concepts about the crucial role of relationship formation in educating children dates back to the early twentieth century. At that time an educator named John Dewey began to discuss educational institutions as "learning communities" (Gabelnick, MacGregor, Matthews, & Smith, 1990). He believed students come to school with a wealth of knowledge and experiences that educators must tap into and utilize in the learning process. In addition, Dewey supported a close relationship between the students and their teachers in the process that he described as "shared inquiry" (Dewey, 1933).

A tremendous amount of research has been gathered over the past one hundred years to determine how young people acquire information.

Over six hundred experimental studies have been done on cooperative, competitive, and individualistic styles of learning (Johnson, Johnson, & Holubec, 1994). The findings from this research have led to the increase of cooperative learning in today's classrooms. Why? *Because positive relationships between students are formed by working cooperatively, and through this cooperation young people have the opportunity to value diversity, find personal and academic support, and experience cohesive as well as productive class environments* (Johnson, Johnson, & Holubec, 1994; Weinstein, 1996).

Sonia Nieto (2000) includes many case studies in her book *Affirming Diversity: The Sociopolitical Context of Multicultural Education.* In her efforts to determine how the needs of today's diverse student population can best be served in institutions of learning, she asked a variety of people to reflect back on their educational experiences. The overwhelming conclusion by these individuals was that when they felt connected to school, they could identify as learners. Nieto concludes that, when young people experience the type of caring environment that permits this connection, they have a far better chance of becoming successful students.

Despite what we already know and are beginning to understand about how vital the formation of positive relationships is for student achievement and satisfaction, we recognize that some of our schools are failing to meet this essential goal. The results of this failure to connect with kids include children who feel disempowered, frustrated, and alienated from the learning experience (Garcia, 2002; Nieto, 2000). Decreased success in school, wide gaps in achievement, and increasing dropout rates have been noted by many educators, and much concern has been raised about how educational institutions are not actively engaging today's students (Banks, 2001; Garcia, 2002; Nieto, 2000; Spring, 2002). Whether due to socioeconomic status, ethnicity, language, or culture, many students are not involved in the "caring communities" that they need in order to connect their real lives to the educational experience.

Although some downplay changing demographics, cultural shifts, and the impacts of globalization as they relate to the shortcomings of the American education system, there have been some major transitions in the United States that cannot and should not be ignored (Berliner &

Biddle, 1995). All of these, along with the increasing knowledge base and escalating demands for the modern workforce, must be taken into account as we redefine what teaching and learning are all about in the twenty-first century.

Yet the core of education must remain consistent: *students are the real reason for teaching!* Their needs *must* be the driving force and focus of learning, and the most basic requirement is that all children have the opportunity to form positive relationships that will allow them to be successful in school, society, and life in general. When young people feel that they have connected with you, the teacher, they will want to learn. They will want to please. They will want to achieve! When students enjoy the classroom environment and their fellow students, they will want to come to school. These kids will also look for opportunities to interact with you and others. They will even become more involved in their school, their community, and the world around them.

As you start to think about whether or not students feel connected to the learning experience at your school, consider the following questions:

- Do the students seem happy to come to your campus? Are they smiling, laughing, energetic, or do they appear to be dragging themselves to school, frowning, discouraged?
- Do the students talk about the curriculum as if it relates to them, or do they seem disinterested in what is being taught?
- Do the young people have a voice on campus? Are their student representatives involved on your school site council, in community forums, or at occasional staff meetings?
- Are there a variety of extracurricular activities for students—from music to sports to clubs? Are all kids encouraged to participate?
- Are many of the various culture groups represented in these activities?

There is no greater reason for learning how to build better relationships in your classroom than to make sure all children feel connected to one another, the curriculum, and the entire learning experience. As I work with preservice teachers, I explain that teaching is like electricity. The power of learning, like this type of energy, is always present, but until you plug into it, you will never see the results of this amazing resource. And this is also true of your students. Unless you, the teacher, reach out and assist them in making the connections needed to be successful, all of that potential energy remains untapped. But prepare yourself—because once you start plugging all of your students into the learning process, anything and everything become possible!

DISCONNECTED TEACHERS CAN'T TEACH

The potential impact that teachers can have in today's diverse classrooms is immeasurable. Perhaps this is one of the reasons that you selected this profession in the first place: *you can make a difference when you touch the life of a child.* Can you imagine how much more the powerful synergy between teaching and learning becomes when the foundation of a great relationship is laid from the very beginning of the school year?

Take a few minutes to think back in your own educational journey to your favorite teacher. Who was he/she? What grade were you in when you had the opportunity of being in his/her class? Why can you still remember this person after all of these years? What did he/she do that made a difference in your life?

I use this reflective activity with every undergraduate and graduate student that I work with, and the answers to these questions, although varying in details, all have a similar theme. The "favorite teacher," whether male or female, young or old, funny or stoic, achieved this status because he or she connected with that student on a deep, personal level.

How about for you? Did this educator touch your life in some significant way—so much so that you think of him or her instantly when this question arises? Actually, I can list several teachers who reached out at different points in my life and not only helped improve the quality of my educational experience during that time but also enhanced my personal life as well. In fact, most of these caring professionals should be credited with guiding me into this career.

The research on educators supports these same findings. Caring, compassionate, and competent teachers positively impact the overall quality of education (Jensen & Kiley, 2000; Wong & Wong, 1998). When professionals in the classrooms put kids first, powerful outcomes are observed both academically and socially (Nieto, 2000; Garcia, 2002). As people in this field improve the quality of the professional connections in their lives, their sense of satisfaction with their careers also increases (Darling-Hammond, Wise, & Klein, 1999; Wong & Wong, 1998).

Unfortunately, many students have experienced the opposite end of the relational spectrum—the burned-out educator who should have left this profession many years ago. Perhaps a painful memory has popped into your thoughts as you read these words. Sadly, you are not alone. There are thousands of young people sitting in classrooms right now listening to someone who has lost his or her joy in teaching. Educating young minds for these individuals has become a process with a pat formula and poor results. The kids aren't fooled, and they know these teachers don't really care about them as individuals—or what they learn or don't learn at school.

What happened to these once idealistic and excited educators? I wish I had a simple answer for that question because then no child would ever have to endure this type of agony and educational malpractice ever again. Research does tell us that difficult work assignments, unclear expectations, inadequate resources, isolation, role conflict, and adjustment problems contribute to teacher burnout and, eventually, attrition (Jensen & Kiley, 2000). Teacher attitudes about their own educational expertise and effectiveness are also key components to their feelings of satisfaction and overall happiness in the profession (Darling-Hammond, Wise, & Klein, 1999).

It is imperative that leaders in the field of education find ways to improve the quality of the educational experience for everyone. *No child should be in a classroom with a teacher who is disconnected from him or her and from the teaching–learning continuum.* It is also unacceptable that we allow educators to ever reach the point where they are worn down, burned out, and dissatisfied with this wonderful career. There must be stop-gap measures in place where teachers, from the very beginning of their careers all the way up to retirement, can ask and receive any and all forms of assistance they need to be productive professionals.

In addition, the attrition rate should be of particular concern in today's educational community. According to statistics, 50 percent of new teachers remain in this profession for less than five years (Jensen & Kiley, 2000). For school systems, this becomes a fiscal as well as a consistency concern. For example, in a district with ten thousand teachers and a turnover rate of even 20 percent, about $500,000 per year could be saved by reducing the attrition by only 1 percent (*Nobscot Corporation, Retention Management and Metrics*, 2002).

As the research on these types of professional dilemmas is evaluated, there appears to be a missing component when it comes to the problem of disconnection in education. What could that piece of the puzzle possibly be? Could it involve assisting new as well as seasoned professionals in learning how to build better relationships? After working in K–12, university, and corporate settings, I can attest to the fact that the personal connections that we form with others are crucial to success in every aspect of life. When a person looks at his or her professional— and personal—life from the perspective of relating, many problems and pitfalls are often avoided or are addressed more easily.

Tragically, there are far too many disconnected teachers. These individuals do not feel good about where they are professionally, and they truly cannot teach students who desperately want someone to relate to on a daily basis. Fortunately, you have an opportunity to never find yourself "unplugged" from your profession—and you have made a good start by simply spending time reflecting about how previous classroom relationships have impacted your own life. The next step in this transformational process will be to discover the other key pieces of the educational puzzle that you will need in order to connect with your students as well as with the dedicated professionals that work all around you.

KEY PLAYERS FOR EDUCATIONAL EXCELLENCE

In *The First Days of Class: A Practical Guide for the Beginning Teacher* (Wilke, 2003), I stress the importance that others play in the ultimate success of the classroom instructor. It is essential not only that teachers know who the key players in education are, but that they also develop healthy relationships with these individuals. As we shall see, this is part of becoming a professional. Most importantly, this process is critical to student learning.

If isolation is indeed one of the major reasons for teacher dissatisfaction as well as attrition, then this should be reason enough for you to investigate how developing relationships with other adults could improve this situation (Jensen & Kiley, 2000). Beginning teachers often experience a reality shock as they adapt to their new profession, adjust to new school cultures, struggle with difficult work assignments, search for resources on a limited budget, and attempt to live up to what are sometimes unclear expectations (Gordon, 1994). Although these are real difficulties, many of them can be confronted by developing connections with other educators who are willing to talk about these problems and help find practical solutions.

The optimal place for a classroom teacher to find a compassionate, supportive comrade is within the ranks of his or her fellow educators. Your colleagues understand exactly where you are in your career—for they are either at that same place (new, progressing, or experienced teachers)—or they have, according to the modern colloquialism, "been there, done that." Experts in the field of education can tell you that taking the initiative to form strong bonds with other teachers will enhance your instructional skills and greatly increase your chances of experiencing professional and personal happiness (Wong & Wong, 1998; Gordon, 1994; Jensen & Kiley, 2000; Wilke, 2003).

Another benefit of building good relationships with colleagues is the added wealth of information that can become part of your own educational "tool kit." For instance, when you have a discipline problem, who better to go to than another experienced educator for ideas on how to deal with the situation? If you are stuck and can't seem to find a creative activity for a particular unit, the teacher across the hall may have the perfect worksheet, lab, or game to fit into your lesson plan. Perhaps you are simply stressed and need someone to listen for a few minutes; why not ask a coworker if you can chat for a few minutes after school—or even buy him a cup of java at the local coffee joint so you have more time to talk? The beauty of this type of connecting is that you will also be the giver of advice, the expert in your subject area, or the shoulder for some other weary professional to cry on. This reaching out is part of what becoming an exceptional educator is all about. (More ideas on how to form these types of positive relationships with your fellow educators will be discussed in chapter 4.)

Your colleagues are also the best source of information on the unique characteristics of your campus. Every workplace has its own culture, and it often takes time for new employees to understand and adapt to the "rites and rituals" of their new environment (Deal & Kennedy,

MULTICULTURAL MATTERS

One of the best ways to connect with your diverse students is to initiate some type of "getting to know you" activity, such as the one below, at the beginning of each school year. Every student in your class comes to school with a treasure chest full of experiences, knowledge, and culture. By learning about one another, both you and your students will begin to understand and appreciate diversity and start building relationships that really do matter!

Getting to Know You

1. My full name is _____, but I like to be called _____.

2. My favorite food is _____.

3. On my days off I like to _____.

4. The best thing about me is _____.

5. _____ is my best friend because _____.

6. My family is great because _____.

7. When I grow up, I'm thinking about becoming a _____ because _____.

8. The most unjust thing in the world to me is _____.

9. If I could help someone in need, I would like to _____.

10. One thing that I would like to do better this year is _____.

11. Is there anything else that you would like me or the class to know about you? _____

1982). There are administrators, secretaries, custodians, classroom aides, and volunteers who will be additional resources to guide you as you learn about your school's unique and dynamic culture. (Chapters 5 and 7 will discuss these key players in the educational arena.)

In particular, educators must be aware of the diversity of today's campuses and classrooms. Not only have the demographics of our student population changed, but also the curriculum, instructional methods, and educational goals are in constant flux (Nieto, 2000; Garcia, 2002; Banks, 2001). And the complexity of schooling cannot be understood outside the context of relationships; it is interactive by its very nature, and this is especially true as we enter the twenty-first century (Nieto, 2000). Indeed, as educational institutions themselves adjust to a changing world, they are discovering that *the single common factor to success is the improvement of relationships* (Fullan, 2001).

As you get to know the key players on your school site, remember that there are other individuals who are invested in the outcomes of education. In addition to parents (see the next section), community members are very concerned about students' success because of their impact upon society (Spring, 2002). This includes businesses that are more involved than ever in supporting education and assisting in the preparation of their future workforce.

With a deeper understanding of the visible and invisible investors in the educational process, you will become a more competent professional. By developing strong connections with your colleagues, you will improve your teaching ability, and this will help you achieve your ultimate goal of helping children thrive in your classroom. The added benefit is that you will also build great relationships that will allow you to feel more satisfied and content both inside and outside of the school setting. Many of the individuals that you are meeting and getting to know right now will work alongside you throughout your career. Take a closer look around you . . . you may actually find friends for a lifetime!

PARENTS—OUR VITAL LINK

Sometimes it is assumed that every teacher automatically understands the importance of the parental role in the education of children, but this can be far from the truth. Yes, educators are aware that mothers and fathers have given birth to, fed, and clothed their children and finally packed a backpack full of goodies for their precious offspring and sent them to the local school, but too many teachers enter the classroom with a vague view of the powerful connection between students and their primary caregivers.

For some teachers, the overwhelming amount of attention that must be given to the curriculum, standards, instructional methods, school-wide goals, discipline guidelines, and the never-ending paper trail totally consumes their thoughts. Time spent thinking about the role that each child's family plays in his or her makeup, learning style, and interactions at school may be minimal at best, but every educator should do this. The instructional manuals need to be set aside—at least for right now. The packet of district standards can be added to the "to do" pile. *One of the first items on your agenda must be contemplating how the parents of your students can, should, and will influence these young lives during the academic year.*

As Wong and Wong (1998) emphasize, parents and caregivers are the first and most influential teachers in children's lives. They are there from the beginning, formulating their initial thoughts and feelings about life and learning. They have impacted everything from the genetic blueprint to the initial imprint of human interactions—and these early connections will forever be a part of what makes each one of your students tick.

In addition to the basic formulation of personality, likes, dislikes, and interests, parents are also the key connection to the cultural nuances of their children. The most obvious is ethnic uniqueness, threads of heritage that have been woven throughout the ages. In addition, language is learned at home. This primary language development is one of the first formal educational experiences a child receives from his or her caregivers (Krashen, 1981). Not only are the skills of communication essential for learning, but they are also at the very foundation of future relationships. All educators in today's diverse classrooms must work diligently to gain a comprehensive understanding of the language abilities and communication styles that students bring to school (Garcia, 2002; Nieto, 2000; Krashen, 1981).

I have observed thousands of parents and caregivers as well as a wide array of parenting styles in my twenty-plus years in education. I've met the overinvolved parent. This is the individual who desires to check on Johnny's progress every day (yes, every single day). I've tried to meet the underinvolved parents, but often they are difficult to track down and do not return phone calls. Luckily, many of my students had balanced, caring, and compassionate caregivers who simply wanted their children to strive to be the best that they could be. Despite these differing parental methods, I have discovered another common theme that can dramatically impact every classroom: *when educators make positive connections with parents, they have powerful allies in the process of teaching and learning.*

Many experts in the field of education agree with this observation. Today, more and more emphasis is being placed on building connections between families, communities, and schools (Comer, Haynes, Joyner, & Ben-Avie, 1996; Darling-Hammond, 1997). By reaching out to these primary caregivers, you can build important bridges to student success as well as stronger, comprehensive, and high-performing school settings (Grissmer, Kirby, Berends, & Williamson, 1994; Garcia, 2002; Darling-Hammond, 1997; Wong & Wong, 1998). The initiation of a positive relationship with parents is the classroom teacher's responsibility. You need to be the one to reach out first—and early—in the school year (Wong & Wong, 1998).

Although there has been much media attention given to supposed public dissatisfaction with education in America, when the evidence is analyzed closely, there are some glaring discrepancies. When adults with school-age children (i.e., those with the most regular contact with public schools) are surveyed, educational institutions are rated highly (Berliner & Biddle, 1995). Indeed, many parents care deeply about their children and would like to stay involved in the academic process, but there are some barriers to their involvement. One of these is the growing number of caretakers across the United States who must work long hours and even two or more jobs in order to support their families. Cultural mismatches and language differences can also be intimidating for many parents (Garcia, 2002; Nieto, 2000). Therefore it should be a major goal of districts, schools, and teachers to remove any obstacle that might keep parents and guardians from interacting with students' academic experiences.

As you become more aware of the way relationships can powerfully impact your own success as an educator, you will also realize how important connecting with your students' parents will be. They truly are your vital link to each child's past, present, and future. (Look for other tips on how to connect with parents, guardians, and caregivers in chapter 6.)

A GLIMPSE INTO THE GLOBAL FUTURE

As you contemplate the critical role that relationships play in your everyday interactions, it becomes increasingly clear that it is crucial to pass the art of connecting with others on to your students. Along with teaching the essential three Rs of education, young people must also know how to formulate and maintain positive connections with their fellow human beings. Although teachers have always had a sense of the "relationship quotient" in education, the transition to a more global community should heighten the commitment to impart these skill sets to the next generation.

Globalization is a term that has been used to describe the expanding connectedness—economic, political, and cultural—of many countries around the world (Nordgren, 2002). Changes in technology and transportation have allowed people to travel and communicate across borders and cultures, and especially in the twenty-first century, the rate of international exchange appears to be increasing exponentially. The concept of globalization and its importance to future generations have been studied and discussed for over a decade, as has the need to improve our educational institutions in order to adjust to these transitions (Snyder, Acker-Hocevar, & Snyder, 1999; Greider, 1997; Micklethwait & Woolbridge, 2000).

From a practical point of view, *teaching students about how to interact, communicate, and collaborate with others will increase their opportunities of success as they enter the job market.* Whether they will acquire jobs with companies in the United States or in international corporations, these future members of the workforce must have the skills necessary to compete in a highly competitive, ever-changing environment (Fullan, 2001; Toffler & Toffler, 1995). By giving them opportunities to be team members in a classroom setting, you will actually be preparing them to interact in whatever corporate culture they choose to work in (Deal & Kennedy, 1982).

Understanding, valuing, and celebrating diversity are also essential in a more global economy. The multicultural nature of American society is evident from small towns to big cities across this vast nation—and it really has been since the founding of this country (Takaki, 1993). Even if students find future employment in companies that service their own communities, they will need to be able to communicate with people from all kinds of backgrounds, cultures, and language experiences. The essential nature of embracing diversity increases exponentially for those young people who plan to become employed internationally. The research on globalization indicates that all members of our workforce must have the ability to deal cooperatively and collaboratively within teams and across cultures (Nordgren, 2002; Fullan, 2001; Toffler & Toffler, 1995).

Educating the next generation about the importance of developing positive relationships in their lives as well as how to attain and sustain these interactions increases the quality of society in general. For the individual, knowing how to relate to others and communicate well aids him or her in achieving tremendous interpersonal success. This success transfers from individual to family to community. In other words, when Juan knows how to make friends, he feels good about himself—and his new friends feel pretty good, too. When Jasmine understands what it means to communicate her feelings in an appropriate way, she can talk to her parents about problems that she's experiencing at school or elsewhere. As the family unit works together to solve Jasmine's problems, the teachers at school can focus more on her academics than on a potential crisis she might have down the road.

This interconnectedness of relationships is like the proverbial pebble that is tossed into a quiet pond. The initial splash seems to be a solitary occurrence, but quickly concentric rings begin to form that move rapidly outward from the place of contact, creating energetic waves that pulsate throughout the formerly still waters. Isn't this the way life is? *People are not isolated islands: our interactions impact one another.* That means what you choose to say and do today can and will impact at least one other person—and possibly more.

And this relationship cycle, like the circle of life, goes on and on. You, the teacher, are part of this process. As you interact with your students, you are teaching them about what *relationship* means. At the same time, your students will be providing you with multiple opportunities to improve and enhance your own communication and interpersonal skills. This is part of your own educational journey. And as you learn more about how to formulate and sustain positive relationships with others, you will not only begin to experience life differently, but you will also be preparing to be part of the global world in which you live.

It took me over ten years of teaching to finally see this bigger picture of education. Perhaps that is why I am so passionate about assisting other educators to grasp the multifaceted nature of relationships and their potential for powerful outcomes both inside and outside of the classroom. No teacher should have to struggle for years trying to discover how to interact and communicate well with students, parents, and coworkers. And no young person should ever graduate from high school without the vital interpersonal skills necessary to assimilate into the job market—as well as into a successful life experience.

Although I have seen the value of great relationship formation repeatedly reinforced over the course of my career, this concept was unequivocally confirmed when I ran into Jason just a few years ago. As a supervisor of student teachers, I often visit various campuses in the southern California area. One Wednesday morning, I waited in line to sign in at the administrative office of a local high school. The student worker who helped with the check-in process and distribution of visitor badges was none other than Jason. Although he was much taller, I recognized his golden locks and impish grin immediately. And yes, he still wore a black T-shirt—although the band name had changed!

"Hi, Mrs. Wilke," he said with a smile.

"Hello, Jason! I'm so glad to see you." And I was. Here he stood, the previously self-professed, chair-throwing student, working in his high school office.

"What have you been up to?" I asked, and he immediately shared some of the details of the past few years. Mostly there were successes, and I was thrilled to hear that he was looking forward to graduation that June. He had made it to his senior year—an achievement that I'm sure some of his previous teachers might have doubted was even possible. Most importantly, he seemed happy and excited about what the future held for him.

I'm not sure what college or career choice Jason has made since our short reunion, but I feel confident in the knowledge that he had gained many of the tools necessary to guide him in whatever he decides to do. Was I part of that process? You bet. And this type of positive result keeps reenergizing my efforts in this amazing profession. Were there others who assisted this young man to get where he is today? Yes! And these caregivers, educators, and community members should feel equally satisfied to have made a difference in even one precious life.

After all, this is what education is all about: *reaching out to others, guiding them down the path toward a better, brighter life, and providing all the tools needed along the way to make this process possible.* I hope that you are beginning to see how relationships can be a vital piece of the educational puzzle, making all the difference in the world to your students—and to your own success within your school community.

CLASSROOM CONUNDRUM

A new teacher on campus comes to you for advice. She is overwhelmed with some aspects of her new job assignment, but her main concern is how to invest time most effectively in regard to the relationships in her life. How much energy should she spend getting to know her students, their parents, and her coworkers? She asks you how she can best prioritize these important connections over the first few months of school so she can also spend time adjusting to the new curriculum, classroom needs, and school culture. What would you recommend? What kind of practical priority list can you provide so that she can begin to formulate and maintain positive relationships both inside and outside of the classroom?

Refer to appendix A, "Potential Solutions for Classroom Conundrums," at the end of the book for ideas on how to answer these questions.

CHAPTER 2

Connecting with Kids in the Diverse Classroom

Nick Whitehead slumped over the hot cup of black coffee, hoping its aromatic steam would stimulate his weary brain cells. It had been an arduous morning, and it was only 10:30 a.m. The faculty lounge was fairly quiet—only a rhythmic hum from the copy machine sounded in the background. As he took a sip of the generic java, he prayed that something—or someone—would give him some inspiration.

Nick's dilemma centered around his first- and second-period ninth-grade English classes. Although he was only two months into his third year at this large, urban high school, he struggled with both groups of adolescents and their lack of interest in reading. Every day was a tedious task of trying to tap into their prior knowledge, create opportunities for active participation, and engage them in stimulating conversation. Like an off-key singer, he felt that everything he tried fell flat. The kids seemed bored, and he was beginning to run out of ideas.

As if his musings had carried to the heavens above, Judy Levine—the school librarian—glided into the faculty lounge and headed toward the pot of hot water near the sink. Watching her grab a mug and open a teabag, Nick rapidly organized his thoughts. Could she hold the key to this Pandora's box? Might Ms. Levine have some fresh ideas on how to get the teenagers' attention?

"Good morning, Judy. Do you have a few minutes? I'd like to ask for your input on a few things," Nick broached cautiously. He really didn't know the librarian too well. Oh sure, they'd talked briefly when he'd brought his students into the library to get books or do research, but he'd been so busy the past few years working with the new curriculum that he hadn't taken the time to really connect with her—or any of the other staff members in the library.

Judy looked in his direction and smiled. Dunking her tea bag in the mug, she walked over and joined him at the large worktable.

"I always have time for teachers," Judy replied kindly, seating herself opposite him. Nick sighed in relief, and he outlined the current status of his classes to her. He had recently introduced a short story by Mark Twain that was set in California as a means of introducing the students to their next novel, *The Adventures of Huckleberry Finn*. Both groups grudgingly read the piece, and most of the students moaned at the mention of this classic novel. Nick shared how he thought the kids would be excited with this famous author because of his sense of humor and colorful American characters.

"Hmm," Judy murmured, casting her gaze toward the ceiling as if she had some ideas tucked away up there. After a few moments of silence, she said, "Nick, you aren't alone in this struggle to get our students excited about reading. I was just talking to another teacher last week about her group of seniors. Part of the problem is the district literature list doesn't excite our diverse student population. But the state Department of Education just sent me its new recommended selections—and many of the contemporary titles include works in Chinese, Filipino, Hmong, Spanish, and Vietnamese."

"But what about teaching the classics like Mark Twain?" Nick queried.

"Oh, we still need to include those great pieces of literature, but by implementing some of these cultural works that today's kids can really relate to, you'll stimulate the initial spark of interest that should get them reading other selections down the road. Here, let me write down the website for you—or you can stop by the library to see our school copy."

After thanking Judy profusely, Nick downed the last drops of coffee and walked with new confidence to his classroom. When the school day ended, he promptly typed www.cde.ca.gov/cl/literature/ into his computer to peruse the suggested titles. In the ninth- to twelfth-grade category, he found numerous suggestions for novels, short stories, and even poetry. After jotting down a few ideas, he headed toward the library to see which ones might be available.

It took a few days to obtain the books he wanted, but his new friendship with Judy Levine helped speed this process. The following Monday, Mr. Whitehead read one of Francisco Jimenez's selections from *The Circuit: Stories from the Life of a Migrant Child*. Many of his Latino students eagerly participated in the discussion that ensued that day. On Tuesday, a handful of these high-schoolers actually volunteered to read sections of another of Jimenez's short stories out loud. Before long, Nick could hardly believe the transformation in these formerly aloof adolescents. They seemed excited to be in his class, and they couldn't wait to talk about the more culturally relevant selections that he had begun to weave into the regular curriculum. And, eventually, these previously resistant students even embraced Huck Finn as part of their reading!

CULTURE COUNTS

Today's educators are not surprised by the cultural diversity on school campuses. In fact, race, ethnic, and language diversity have always been part of the unique and rich history of this nation (Banks, 2001; Spring, 2002; Wilke, 2003). The changing demographics of our student population simply mirrors the "deepening ethnic texture of the United States" (Banks, 2001, p. xxi). With these enriched and diverse "textures," however, come a variety of concerns, dilemmas, and opportunities that school communities must adequately address to ensure academic equity for all children.

At the very foundation of the discussion about diversity in twenty-first-century schools is the concept of culture. Culture by definition includes the "intangible, symbolic, and ideational aspects of group life" (Banks, 2001, p. 70). It is a methodology or system of understanding society or a subgroup of society (Banks, 2001; Garcia, 2002; Deal & Kennedy, 1982; Nieto, 2000) to which individuals belong, and it includes things such as:

- values
- beliefs
- knowledge
- symbols

- myths
- law
- customs
- language

It is essential for educators to understand that every individual has his or her own unique culture. When they consider how best to identify and relate to the cultural backgrounds of students, teachers must realize that they themselves approach life from their own cultural experiences as well. In addition, experts poignantly note that every organization also has its own culture (Deal & Kennedy, 1982). Therefore the process of educating young people involves culturally aware teachers addressing the needs of many individuals from diverse cultures, all within the culture of a particular school, district, and community. Although these multifaceted concepts may seem like a spider's web of potential problems, they can also be perceived as threads that may weave a richly diverse tapestry. What is needed, however, is thoughtful planning, effort, and flexibility by everyone involved.

Unfortunately, during most of the twentieth century, educational institutions struggled with comprehending how essential these cultural nuances were and how best to implement a curriculum that could meet all of the diverse needs within their circle of influence (Banks, 2001; Spring, 2002; Wilke, 2003). Many of the instructional methods utilized in schools were simply unsuccessful in connecting with how ethnically diverse children acquired and retained information (Darling-Hammond, 1997). These communication mismatches resulted in culture conflicts and, ultimately, school failure (Nieto, 2000).

Thankfully, there are signs of improvement in regard to embracing cultural differences as well as meeting the needs of all students in today's school communities. Many educators are attempting to understand how various culture groups teach their youth and are researching improved instructional methods and curriculum that will engage young people in the teaching–learning continuum. As a classroom teacher, you have the opportunity to improve the cultural interactions within your classroom on a daily basis. First, you can begin to analyze your own culture and its impact on how you share knowledge and information with others. Second, you can also evaluate the culture of your school to discover how it meets—and does not meet—the needs of the young people who make up its community.

Making culture count starts with awareness, but the next move toward educational excellence is ensuring that everyone has an opportunity to learn at his or her own optimum level. This isn't an easy task because it includes knocking down the standard approach to teaching in more or less an "assembly line" method and restructuring the process of educating young minds with more of an individualistic approach (Spring, 2002). The overall goal is to make certain that what is taught in school (both tangible and intangible) is "culturally compatible, culturally congruent, culturally appropriate, culturally responsive, [and] culturally relevant" (Nieto, 2000, p. 149).

If you want to truly connect with the kids in your classroom, you must first understand their cultures—as well as your own! Nick Whitehead quickly discovered that teaching his students became a whole lot easier, more efficient, and more effective when he addressed their backgrounds, learning styles, and interests. It took some extra effort on his part; he had to reach out for help as well as do some additional research. He also had to step outside the educational box a bit and look beyond the standard curriculum. Yet his efforts paid off exponentially—especially when it came to his own understanding about how he approached teaching and learning.

You will make a difference with young people when you show you care about who they are as individuals, and this includes the culture that they come from. As you contemplate the educational process that is taking place in your classroom and around your campus, be open to new ideas and ways of thinking about your own cultural experiences and how they impact the students in your diverse classroom. Remember, culture is dynamic, complex, and changing, so that means that educators can—and should—evolve too (Banks, 2001; Garcia, 2002).

THE EMOTIONAL QUOTIENT—HOW DO I RELATE?

If we took time to review the American educational system over the past two centuries, the importance of the three Rs—reading, 'riting, and 'rithmetic—would be evident in everything from curriculum to instructional methodology. Not only do we teach in these major areas of learning, but we test in them as well. For instance, the Wechsler Intelligence Scale was developed and introduced in 1939 by David Wechsler in order to hone in on the "global nature of intelligence" (Jensen & Kiley, 2000). The level of achievement on this type of examination provides information about IQ, or the intelligence quotient/potential of children. Since the original Wechsler, many norm-referenced tests have been developed and implemented in schools, and these exams have become big business in education (Spring, 2002).

During the latter half of the twentieth century, some educators reevaluated the traditional assessment of intelligence as well as the methods being utilized to teach children. One researcher, Howard Gardner, studied and reported on a new approach in understanding the ways kids learn—and how educators can help all students achieve at their maximum potential within academic settings. In addition to including the mathematical and verbal abilities of individuals, which are typically addressed under the "IQ" domain, Gardner's theory of multiple intelligences incorporates five other means by which people acquire information (Gardner, 1983). In the past few years, Gardner and others have expanded on these concepts and added two other types of "intelligences" to the original seven (Gardner, 1999; Armstrong, 1999).

Interpersonal and intrapersonal intelligences are two of the areas within the theory of multiple intelligences that help explain how some individuals process information. Thomas Armstrong (1999) simplifies the two categories into "people smart" and "self smart." During the 1990s, John Mayer and Peter Salovey combined these two intelligences into the term EQ, or "emotional quotient," and then, in 1995, Daniel Goleman wrote *Emotional Intelligence: Why It Can Matter More than IQ*. The basic premise behind his research is that a person's ability to understand his or her own emotions and the emotions of others is equally important as (if not more than) a high score on an IQ exam.

Everyone has EQ potential, just as we have an IQ. And, just as people are gifted in various areas of traditional intelligence, they are also blessed with some qualities within the emotional intelligences domain. For example, many teachers rate highly on tests that assess *interpersonal* intelligence, and they can concur with a statement such as "I enjoy the challenge of teaching another person, or groups of persons, what I know how to do" (Armstrong, 1999, pp. 21–22). A person with strengths in the area of *intrapersonal* intelligence can relate to statements such as "I have opinions that set me apart from the crowd" or "I have some important goals for my life that I think about on a regular basis" (Armstrong, 1999, pp. 22–23).

When you look at the world from the perspective of relationships, you will understand the positive impact that improved emotional intelligence can have in homes, schools, communities, and workplaces. The ability to get along with others is a basic component of EQ. Excellent communication skills as well as accurate assessment of personal responses and reactions of others are integral components to personal and professional success. *Great leaders and communicators have the ability to understand who they are as well as how important the feelings, hopes, and dreams of others around them are.*

Research reveals the benefits of identifying and working on strengths as well as weaknesses related to one's emotional quotient. These include:

- improvement in recognizing one's emotions
- increased understanding about feelings
- distinguishing between feelings and actions
- better frustration levels and improved anger management
- decreased verbal attacks, fighting, and classroom behavior problems
- decline in aggressive and self-destructive behavior
- more positive feelings about self, school, and family (Goleman, 1995)

It is vital that you, the educator, evaluate your own abilities when it comes to interpersonal and intrapersonal intelligence. As these researchers have pointed out, an amazing aspect of this new way of looking at intelligences is that weak areas can be improved upon once they are identified. There are specific strategies that you can employ to improve your EQ level, and the ability to know more about yourself will serve you well in all aspects of life (Gardner, 1999; Armstrong, 1999).

As with all areas of self-awareness and growth, what you do as a teacher can't help but positively influence your students as well. In order to achieve at their maximum potential, kids need to believe that you

MULTICULTURAL MATTERS

Helping your students learn more about one another is a perfect way to start developing good relationships in the classroom. RQ skills can be learned, so how about trying a few of these "relationships builders" when you can fit them—and others like them—into the curriculum!

"Tell Me More about You"

Elementary school: Put your students' names up on a bulletin board in an acrostic style so that next to each letter you can list qualities about that student for everyone to see. For example, BRAD = Bold, Reliable, Athletic, Determined. Later, have the students bring in a picture or item that can be hung next to their names. This will allow their classmates to know more about who they are or what things they like!

Middle school: Using the same acrostic concept above, have students work in small groups to come up with name tags of their own to display. Give them some guidelines as well as a list of potential positive characteristics. Next, have the groups post these on a bulletin board as they share with the rest of the class. Finally, purchase a disposable camera and take pictures of your students—then put these fun photos up by their name-tag display.

High school: Let your students have an interview day, where they are assigned classmates to get to know better. You can provide a preprinted sheet of questions or even have the students devise questions of their own. Be sure to give plenty of time for them to share the new things they learned about one another with the entire class, then post the interview sheets up somewhere in your room.

---

care about them on a personal level, and they will also be able to grasp the importance of improving their own EQ as they watch you role model vital aspects of it every day (Mendler, 2001). What could be better than teaching young people how to communicate well, care about others, and appreciate who they are as individuals?

As you connect with the students who make up the diverse classroom and community you work in, you will quickly discover how EQ affects learning as well as every aspect of the relationships that you are developing. James Comer stresses the importance of improving interpersonal connections in the educational reform process. He sums up these thoughts succinctly: "I have often said that relationships are to development what location is to real estate. We need relationship, relationship, relationship"(Comer, Ben-Avie, Haynes, & Joyner, 1999, p. xxiv).

IT'S ELEMENTARY

I recently spent an interesting morning volunteering in my niece's kindergarten classroom. Perhaps there is no better setting than an elementary school to see at work all the goals, hopes, dreams, and aspirations that American education comprises. Within the walls of this busy room were two exuberant teachers and thirty-two active four-, five-, and six-year-olds. Every minute was packed with high-quality teaching and hands-on experiences. The environment felt safe and inviting, and each detail, from the colorful rug to the creative charts, inspired the children to engage in active learning.

What most impressed me during this visit was how eager young children are to interact with anyone and everyone who enters their environment. Even as the teachers introduced me to the class, I noticed many youngsters smile and wave at me. Others had curious expressions on their faces as if to say, "Who are you, and why are you in my classroom?" Soon the students broke into smaller groups and moved to several workstations. When I also went to the table I was assigned to assist, two girls immediately asked my name again and wanted me to know theirs as well. A shy boy at the end of the table caught my attention, so I walked over to check his work. When he wouldn't say his name, a friend next to him shared, "He's Joel." I spent a few more minutes asking Joel some questions, and he slowly began to smile and share a little bit more about the picture he had been drawing.

It didn't take too much effort to form a simple relationship with Joel—and, for that matter, the other kindergarten students in this class at Conway Elementary School. They seemed more than willing to welcome me into their room, and when it was time for me to leave, several asked when I'd be back again. This type of warm response shouldn't surprise anyone who knows about child development. The social development of what we term "early-to-middle childhood" involves burgeoning social skills, particularly as kids move away from home and into more socially interactive settings such as school (Kaluger & Kaluger, 1979). As students enter the schooling experience, they start to learn about age-appropriate roles, communication skills, social interactions, and understanding the needs and rights of those around them (Kaluger & Kaluger, 1979).

As an elementary school educator, it is important to note that children start kindergarten with a wide array of abilities when it comes to interacting with others. As previously discussed, some individuals naturally possess a high level of emotional intelligence (Armstrong, 1999; Gardner, 1999). Those youngsters already seem to understand their own feelings and are often quite sensitive to the emotions and needs of those around them (Doty, 2001). Others, however, not only may have strengths in other areas of intelligence (and not especially in emotional intelligence), but they also may not have had the "cradle to school" experiences that develop their emotional quotient (Sprenger, 2002).

Research confirms that children reach middle childhood with an awareness of self-esteem and self-concept developed directly from their parents, family members, and peer group (Kaluger & Kaluger, 1979). The connection between the type of home environment a child comes from and his or her behavior is also extremely powerful. For instance, if a boy or girl has been raised in a household that has a dominating parent, this student may be shy, submissive, self-conscious, uncooperative, bold, quarrelsome, or disinterested in learning. If, however, children experience a calm, harmonious home life, they are more likely to be cooperative and independent and show good adjustment skills in a variety of situations (Kaluger & Kaluger, 1979).

Within an elementary school setting you will discover numerous ways in which children interact with adults and one another. *Although we can control neither the life experiences of children before they begin school nor what occurs after the school day has ended, educators can provide many opportunities within the classroom to improve social interactions, relationship formation, and emotional intelligence in general.* Perhaps the best news of all is that these are not "extras" that must be added on to an already full curriculum. Instead, this is a process of learning that children are already wired to acquire (Doty, 2001; Kaluger

& Kaluger, 1979). Everything, from teaming to play groups, journaling to playground games, class discussions to role-modeling, can promote opportunities to learn about how healthy relationships are formed and maintained over time (Sprenger, 2002; Doty, 2001).

MEETING IN THE MIDDLE

For some educators, middle-schoolers are the most marvelous individuals on earth. These blooming adolescents have high energy and enthusiasm that can help create dynamic classrooms where a tremendous amount of learning takes place. Yet not everyone is up to the task of captivating the interest of these rapidly transforming minds and bodies—and sometimes this even includes the parents! Adolescence is a challenging time for everyone involved—and especially for the students who are developing from children into young adults before our very eyes. Indeed, the term *adolescence* itself comes from the Latin verb *adolescere*, which means to grow into maturity (Kaluger & Kaluger, 1979).

Because of the obvious physical changes that are taking place during this maturing process, educators must be cognizant of the psychological implications for behavior. Young people are often highly self-conscious during the middle school years, and one of their biggest fears is to stand out in any way from their peer group (Kaluger & Kaluger, 1979). Sometimes the hormonal fluctuations for both boys and girls impact their emotions and how they relate to those around them, but it is important that adults not stereotype all adolescents with preconceived notions about how they may or may not act based on their age alone (Santrock, 1983). As with individuals of all ages, there are many variations in behavior, but the changes taking place in these young people are more evident because transitions seem to occur in such a short period of time.

Having taught in middle school for over ten years, I can assure you that it is a dynamic work environment that will provide excitement and variety in your professional life. Some days I would completely revamp my plans because the students' interests and needs had shifted. When middle-schoolers develop a passion for learning about something, they often do so with abandon—and I quickly discovered that it was best to harness this enthusiasm rather than put a damper on the students' energy level. Probably the greatest lesson that I learned, however, was how essential building relationships could be with students in this age group.

The reasons for creating positive connections within the middle school environment are numerous, but perhaps the most important is that the relationships you develop actually create an atmosphere of trust that will allow students to relax and want to learn anything that you have to share with them (Mender, 2001). In addition, as you foster the formation of good relationships within your classroom environment, behavior management problems tend to decrease at a noticeable rate (Weinstein, 1996). What educator wouldn't want this to happen in his or her classroom?

After the foundation of relationships has been laid, educators can then address academic strategies that will encourage students to succeed. When young people see that you care about them, that you believe they can achieve, and that you desire the best for them, they will almost always strive to fulfill your expectations (Mendler, 2001; Weinstein, 1996; Wilke, 2003). Unfortunately, some people still operate under the assumption that learning will take place at school simply because students are present. Today more and more educators are discovering that kids—especially adolescents—don't always subscribe to this same belief. *Many students want educators to show them why they should care about learning, and if you offer them a very good reason, they will often step up to the plate—ready to play right alongside you!*

Once these simple, yet personal, connections have been made with your students, you'll then be able to add the final dimension to the educational experience: teaching young people how to improve their own relationships with one another. Middle-schoolers are naturally wired to be social, and they are at the stage of life where they are very interested in peer relationships (Kaluger & Kaluger, 1979). Along with this comes a natural desire to be emancipated from the home, and this can include some antagonism toward parents and adults in general (Kaluger & Kaluger, 1979; Santrock, 1983). Middle school teachers need to be aware of this normal part of development and work toward building positive relationships with their students, despite periods that might be more difficult than others.

Because of middle-schoolers' increased interest in social development, this is an ideal time to incorporate group learning experiences and interactions within your classroom. Cooperative learning is an exceptional method that engages students in the learning process, plus it has an added bonus of giving young people opportunities to talk and socialize during appropriate times in class (Weinstein, 1996; Wilke, 2003). In addition, by allowing your students to connect with one another, you will help them break down barriers that tend to divide students at this age level as well as provide them with the skills needed to learn how to connect with people who may be different than they are (Mendler, 2001).

HIGH-ENERGY HIGH SCHOOLS

If you haven't been on a high school campus in some time, you might feel overwhelmed by the rapid daily pace of middle to late adolescence. There is a tremendous amount going on in twenty-first-century high schools, including increased academic pressures to meet higher standards set by school districts, states, and federal agencies as well as by colleges and businesses. Weinstein (1996) describes the secondary classroom: "It is more like a subway or a bus than a place designed for learning, and it is hard to think of another setting (except prison, perhaps) where such large groups of individuals are packed so closely together for so many hours" (p. 3).

Yet high schools are also a place where many fabulous experiences occur—for students and educators alike. This is the final preparation stage for life in the real world, and many teachers are assisting young people to prepare for higher academic experiences and for their future careers. Because of the students' increased cognitive abilities and readiness for divergent ways of thinking and reasoning, deeper levels of learning can be attained (Kaluger & Kaluger, 1979; Santrock, 1983). In addition, the questioning of values, morals, and standard ways of thinking by many adolescents allows for in-depth discussions within today's classrooms (Kaluger & Kaluger, 1979).

Although the unique opportunity to work with older adolescents is exciting for many educators, there are also some real problems that they, like their students, must contend with on a daily basis. First, high schools are often crowded places that offer few places for quiet reflection or privacy (Weinstein, 1996). In addition, secondary settings not only operate at a rapid pace, but they are also places of immediacy and unpredictability where situations arise at a moment's notice—such as an argument or physical conflict—that must be dealt with quickly and efficiently. School assemblies or pep rallies might be added to what was once a normal day without any prior notice, and everyone must rework their schedules around these types of changes (Weinstein, 1996; Wilke, 2003).

The bottom line is that high schools of the twenty-first century are multidimensional environments where many things are taking place at once, much like the real world into which these young people will soon take their first steps. *It is up to educators not only to help students adjust to the high school experience but also to give them the skills necessary to achieve within an ever-changing global community.*

Once again, the connections that you make with your students at this age level will be vital for their development as well as the climate within your classroom. You should be aware that your high school students will be at different stages of adolescence, therefore their physical, emotional, and mental development will vary accordingly. There will still be a continued need to individuate while at the same time fit into a peer group (Kaluger & Kaluger, 1979; Santrock, 1983). Conflicts with caregivers and other adults are not uncommon, yet your students will also be looking for teachers who show helping, friendly, and understanding behavior as well as leadership skills (Weinstein, 1996). And, like middle-schoolers, they will naturally desire a great deal of social contact with their fellow students.

As you strive toward building good relationships with your students, you'll discover that many aspects of the educational experience seem to fall naturally into place. The students will be happier and want to come to school when they feel connected with you, their other teachers, and their fellow students. Once they have formed positive relationships, kids will want to get involved on campus as well as achieve more and more. Finally, as you model how to interact well with others, the young people in your class will begin to acquire the skills necessary to survive and thrive in the world around them, especially when they know how to positively connect with others on a day-to-day basis.

CLASSROOM CONUNDRUM

You have a student this year who seems to be very withdrawn and isolated from his classmates. You've tried various seating arrangements and even encouraged a few of your more social students to welcome him into their groups. Unfortunately, all of your efforts seem to be failing, and recently you have noticed his grades dropping. Now every time you attempt to talk to him personally, he seems to rebuff your efforts. Despite your desire to help, you also have thirty other students who need your attention, and some of them are actually pleasant and appreciative when you interact with them. How do you continue to foster the energy to assist this one seemingly disinterested student? Are there more steps that you could take, or should you try to enlist someone else to help at this point?

Refer to appendix A, "Potential Solutions for Classroom Conundrums," at the end of the book for ideas on how to answer these questions.

CHAPTER 3

Connecting with Special Kids

As I took roll one September morning, I paused to survey my class of sixth graders with pleasure. They were working diligently on their morning journal, an activity that I opened the day with so that they could express their thoughts and ideas on a chosen topic. I had already grown to like this bunch of bright eleven- and twelve-year-olds; as a group they seemed to have a unique zest for learning. As I smiled at the scene of learners in action, my gaze suddenly fell upon Kelly, a sweet, quiet girl who sat in the front row. She was staring into space with a glazed expression across her face.

I quickly finished the attendance duties and walked over to see how I could help get her back on task. Perhaps she was tired or hadn't slept well. Many of the students I had in this large middle school were involved in extracurricular activities, so it wasn't unusual for a few of them to drift off in these early morning hours.

"Kelly, is everything okay?" I queried.

"Oh yes, Mrs. Wilke," she said in her usual soft tone, "I was just thinking about the question you have on the board. I don't really understand it."

I glanced at the prompt I had written on the front white board. It was a fairly straightforward question: "What's your opinion about the school's new lunch policy? Have things been easier or more difficult during your lunch hour with this system?"

"What question can I help you with?" I asked, glancing down at the empty page where she was tapping her pencil.

"Well, what's the word *policy* mean? And, I'm not sure how to explain what I think about lunchtime."

I looked into Kelly's blue eyes, realizing that the lost look was quite sincere. I explained how the school was trying to make things easier by helping with the long lines outside the cafeteria—something that we had discussed as a class the preceding week when the new system was first implemented. I asked Kelly if she remembered that discussion, but she shook her head. Once I was sure that she had a few ideas and had started to write some of them down, I moved on to check on my other students' progress.

Yet Kelly's comprehension problem raised a warning flag in the back of my mind. I decided to keep a close watch on her work during the upcoming week. It didn't take long for another incident to occur. The following day, I again caught Kelly staring off into space, this time during a math assignment. All of her classmates had easily grasped the concepts, then started the worksheet I had assigned, so I made my way to Kelly's desk and knelt down next to her.

"Can I help you with the worksheet?" I whispered.

"Yeah, I don't get it," she replied, looking down into her lap.

"Did you understand the lesson when I went over it?"

"Well, kind of—I got a little lost toward the end."

"Don't forget you can stop me and ask questions any time you aren't following what I'm saying. Now, let's look at a few of these problems."

As I went through the worksheet with Kelly, I noted that she struggled with some basic multiplication procedures. When I asked her how she'd done in math the year before, she smiled sweetly and said "Okay." I desperately wanted to believe her, but the facts on the sheet in front of me did not confirm her statement.

During my break that afternoon, I stopped by the office to look in Kelly's cumulative file. None of my records indicated that she had any special needs, but instinct and experience made me concerned that maybe she was one of those students who truly had "slipped through the cracks." The cumulative folder showed pictures of this precious child from kindergarten on, as well as records of grades and evaluations from her previous teachers. As I poured over the records on Kelly from the time she entered school, my heart rate quickened. Each year the educator had noted "slowness" and "struggles in some subjects," but they had also mentioned that Kelly "really tries" and that "she should do better next year with more maturity." Year after year, however, her grades were poor, and there was no sign that any special testing had ever been done.

At that point, I was convinced that there was more to be concerned with, and that at sixth grade we had no more time to wait for maturity. Kelly was behind, and she would probably fall further and further behind in the rapid pace of middle and high school. After replacing this folder, I walked across the hall to speak to one of the school counselors.

It took a few weeks, but after contacting Kelly's parents and setting up a battery of tests, I determined that Kelly indeed had a learning disability. The counselor was able to place her in a resource class for two periods a day, and I was able to work with her for the rest of her school hours. After a few months of this extra assistance, I noticed tremendous improvement in Kelly's ability to focus as well as in some of her basic skill areas, such as math and writing. She participated more and even seemed to have greater self-esteem.

An additional bonus came across my desk midyear in the form of a note from Kelly's mother. After our efforts with Kelly, she had become concerned about one of her other daughter's difficulties in school. She decided to be proactive and ask the elementary school to test Kaitlyn, who was found to have the same learning disability Kelly had. Now Kaitlyn would have a chance to get the help she needed well before she entered middle school.

ALL KIDS ARE SPECIAL

While no one in the field of education ever wants to hear about a child who slips through the cracks for as long as Kelly did, this scenario occurs over and over again. Fortunately, with increased knowledge and training, teachers are better able to assess the needs of students and find ways to help every young person achieve to the best of his or her ability. As we have discussed, one of the optimum ways to do this is to start the school year off learning everything that you can about each and every one of your students.

As you survey your own classroom, realize that the students already come to you with a wealth of information and experiences. Whether they are kindergartners or seniors in high school, they have a trunkload of knowledge about the world in which they have journeyed thus far.

They have ideas about people, places, and things. Many of these will be powerful and positive concepts; a few, however, may be negative. *It is the job of educators to tap into this wealth of resources and begin to understand how unique and special all students truly are* (Wilke, 2003).

In fact, one of the best mottoes to have in the field of education is "all kids are special." And they are! Each and every one has talents, abilities, and unique characteristics that set them apart from any other person on the planet. Even as you look at students' handicaps or disabilities, you will find strengths that would more than likely not be present without the other issues they must deal with in their lives.

The theory of multiple intelligences reveals that every individual has strengths that can be identified, developed, and enhanced over time (Gardner, 1983, 1999). Armstrong (1999) describes these intelligences as word smart, picture smart, music smart, body smart, logic smart, people smart, and self smart. Two areas that researchers are currently investigating are the naturalist and the existential intelligences (Gardner, 1999).

The crux of this theory is that everyone has areas of strength and abilities—probably two or three, but maybe even more. In addition, people have at least one area of weakness, but human beings have the ability to improve in these areas as well (Gardner, 1983; Armstrong, 1999). For example, someone who is strong in mathematical and logic skills but lacking in musical ability can improve the latter intelligence by increasing his or her exposure to music. This could mean listening to classical tunes, attending concerts, or taking lessons with a musical instrument. Exposure and experience are essential to improving any of the skills that may be lacking in a particular intelligence.

Educators must identify and accentuate the multiple intelligences of young people. Not only do these aspects make students special, but they also provide opportunities for success both inside and outside of the educational experience. Testing that is done for children will help identify some of their academic strengths, but standardized exams do not reveal the entire picture about an individual child (Spring, 2002). Indeed, some researchers are concerned that standardized testing can actually be a disservice to many children, particularly minority students (Darling-Hammond, 1997; Nieto, 2000; Spring, 2002).

Kelly provides a perfect example of the concept that all kids are indeed special. Although she had a definite learning disability that had kept her from achieving at her optimum level before she received additional assistance, she always excelled when it came to the RQ. Each morning Kelly arrived with a smile on her face and a friendly hello. She interacted with her peers and with adults extremely well, and she was well liked by everyone around her. Kelly was the first to notice if someone was down or discouraged, and she usually tried to engage that person in a conversation, despite her own quiet nature.

Indeed, it may have been Kelly's strong abilities when it came to "people smartness" and her outstanding emotional intelligence that kept her learning disability from being identified early on in her educational experience. Because she was so pleasant and willing to please, she apparently was passed from grade to grade in the hope that someday she would catch up with everyone else. In other words, her outstanding RQ also covered up some serious weaknesses! As a teacher, it is particularly important to be cognizant of the mixed blessings when it comes to your students' gifts. When assessing students, you not only need to discover their strengths and weaknesses, but you should also look for areas that may be compensating for or camouflaging problems that could hurt them further along in their educational journey.

STRUGGLES WITH SLOWER LEARNERS

As any teacher can tell you, discovering how to pace a lesson so that all students are acquiring the information adequately is a difficult task. One reason for this may be obvious: every classroom contains a group of students who learn in a variety of ways. Although teachers must address learning styles as they prepare daily lessons, they must also keep all of their students actively engaged, on task, and synchronized in the learning process.

How can this be done effectively and efficiently? To begin with, you must remember two simple yet essential facts of the education process:

- All students can learn!
- All students learn at different rates.

Educators may intellectually grasp the notion that children and young people learn differently, yet for some reason, when they enter their classrooms, they tend to teach to "the group." As Spring (2002) describes it, educational institutions become more like factories with an assembly-line system. What works for most must work for all, right? Wrong! This may be true for cars and washing machines, but it is certainly not for human beings. You might try sending your students down the same track, but more than likely chaos will erupt before too long. The gifted children will be as frustrated as those who learn at slower rates.

And we wonder why we have trouble keeping some of our students achieving—let alone succeeding—at school! In fact, when slower learners can't keep up, they often quit altogether. So what is an educator to do with slower-learning students when the pressure of increased standards and accountability, as well as the very real difficulty of keeping the regular and fast-learning students on task, weighs heavily on his or her mind?

The most important goal must be to help all of your students learn how to learn (Joyce & Weil, 1996). If young people can acquire the skills to identify what is essential for them to know, how best to take that information in, and how to communicate that back in an effective manner, you will have provided them with the educational tools that will last a lifetime. For the slower learner, this critical skill will probably be attained at a slower pace—but it can and must be learned. Exceptional educators and educational institutions must provide all students with the basic tools to grasp academic information as quickly and as efficiently as possible (Joyce & Weil, 1996; Wong & Wong, 1998).

As you aid these slower-learning students as they "learn how to learn," they will begin to understand why they need to acquire information in the first place. This process involves time—and lots of it. No matter what subject area you teach, if you increase the amount of time that the students actually work on the lesson, you will increase learning (Wong & Wong, 1998). In addition, the more actively you engage all of your kids in the educational process, the greater the chances are that they will absorb what is being taught (Jensen & Kiley, 2000; Wong & Wong, 1998).

When assisting the slower students in your class, you will notice that they tend to need more support and guidance than your speedier students. This is a perfect opportunity for you to have these faster-learning kids help their classmates. In addition, if you employ a variety of cooperative learning activities, you will have the freedom to become more of a facilitator in your classroom, moving around and checking on the progress of all your students (Johnson, Johnson, & Holubec, 1994).

The fact that you have slower-learning students in your classroom may also encourage you to find outside support for them. For instance, you may decide to include parents and volunteers who want to be involved in the local schools (see chapters 6 and 7 for more ideas). Your campus may already have an organized volunteer program. If not, perhaps this is an activity that you might take on yourself to become more involved at school and in the community.

Remember, these slower learners will be like all of your other students in that they, too, will have multiple intelligences working in their favor. However, they will need your assistance and support to discover how to apply these strengths within the learning environment, where they may not have been very successful in the past. *As an exceptional educator, you must check, double-check, and then check again to be certain that all of your students are acquiring the information necessary for them to achieve not only in your class but also in the future.*

LOOKING AT LEARNING DISABILITIES

Although our educational system certainly needs improvement in some areas in order to meet the needs of today's diverse students, it has been a tremendous source of support and compassion for children across America. Few nations attempt to provide thirteen years of free education for every child within its borders, including those with disabilities (Smith, Polloway, Patton, & Dowdy, 2001). During the second half of the twentieth century, the efforts to identify and assist those with special needs increased dramatically, revealing the dedication that parents, educators, and community members have to ensuring that all children receive an excellent educational experience (Shea & Bauer, 1997).

The subject of learning disabilities often seems very broad and ambiguous, even to professionals in the field of education. Special needs students will fit into one of these areas:

- learners with disabilities
- learners with learning disabilities
- learners who are gifted, creative, or talented (Shea & Bauer, 1997)

Students who fall into any of these categories have specific needs that must be addressed both inside and outside of the classroom environment. As an exceptional educator, it is imperative that you become more aware of the variety of learning needs that you will encounter during the course of your career.

Students identified as having learning disabilities are among the largest and fastest growing group in the field of special education (Smith, Polloway, Patton, & Dowdy, 2001; Shea & Bauer, 1997). A learning disability is described as a discrepancy between ability and achievement. An example of a student with a learning disability would be a sixth grader who reads only at a second-grade level; in this instance, testing and other evaluations would be done to ensure that no underlying factor was involved in this discrepancy. In other words, if the reading deficiency is caused by a hearing or visual problem, the student might not fit the definition for "learning disabled" (LD), but instead would have other special needs that must be assessed (Shea & Bauer, 1997).

Learning disabilities can include Attention Deficits and Hyperactivity (ADHD), memory problems, cognition deficits, perceptual differences, as well as motor skill and coordination difficulties. Parents or teachers often identify students with disabilities in the early years of life; yet it is still important for all educators to be observant. Students who are struggling to grasp concepts and do not seem to be doing well must be given extra attention. Kelly had slipped through six years of the educational system before she was ever tested!

When it comes to identifying those with learning disabilities, there is growing concern among educators about how to accurately test culturally and linguistically diverse students (Smith, Polloway, Patton, & Dowdy, 2001). Unfortunately, research reveals that there are a disproportionate number of minority students being placed in special education programs rather than receiving help in other areas that might be holding them back—such as English language acquisition (Moecker, 1992). Some educational experts conclude that this may be due to inappropriate teacher viewpoints about who should be given this type of placement (Smith, Polloway, Patton, & Dowdy, 2001). As we discussed in chapter 2, the cultural diversity of today's classroom is increasing; but students should not be put in special education simply because they may still be acquiring English language skills!

MULTICULTURAL MATTERS

Special needs kids often feel they are different than the rest of their peers. One way to help create an atmosphere of inclusion in your classroom is to provide opportunities for young people to discover what they have in common. An activity such as a personal time capsule is an easy way to give your students a chance to find out more about themselves and one another—as well as to see just how similar they really are!

Personal Time Capsule

Below please list ten items that you would select to put in a time capsule that will be opened one hundred years from now. Remember that these things will be the only clues that the people in 2104 will have to get to know who you were as a person in 2004!

1. _____

2. _____

3. _____

4. _____

5. _____

6. _____

7. _____

8. _____

9. _____

10. _____

If you'd like, bring in one or two items from your list to share with the class!

Educational research also shows that students who have been identified with learning disabilities often struggle in areas of self-esteem as well as in their interactions with others. Social competence and behavior problems are not uncommon with these learners, and even signs of withdrawal and depression have been observed (Shea & Bauer, 1997). *Although we must be careful with generalizations, it is apparent that young people with learning disabilities may need much more attention from the caring adults in their lives as well as specific skills for building and fostering good relationships.*

In *The First Days of Class: A Practical Guide for the Beginning Teacher*, educators were reminded how crucial it is to be aware of students' special needs—especially those with learning disabilities (Wilke, 2003). Not only will it be important for you to read all information provided to you by the counselors, school psychologist, and other specialists regarding children who will be in your class, but it is also essential that you attend any and all meetings for these students. As you do so, you will no doubt discover additional ways to improve the quality of instruction for these special children.

SPECIAL NEEDS

In addition to students who have learning disabilities, educators will also encounter a variety of children throughout their professional experience who have specific physical, mental, emotional, and behavioral needs—or any combination of these. For instance, there are learners with mild or moderate mental retardation, sensory impairments, autism, communication disorders, and mild to severe disabilities (Shea & Bauer, 1997). Although these students will be receiving some support through a special education program on campus, they may also be mainstreamed into the traditional classroom in what is called "inclusive settings" (Smith, Polloway, Patton, & Dowdy, 2001).

Students with special needs usually excel when they work with compassionate, caring educators, so don't be worried about being able to teach them simply because you haven't had specific coursework or preparation in the area of special education. Your coworkers who have specialized in this field will be more than willing to assist you in acquiring the tools and techniques to include these young people in your classroom setting. Over the years I have had a number of special needs children in my classes, and I look back on these experiences with fondness. I learned more about living life to the fullest from many of these kids than I have from any other person I've encountered. In addition, by having special-needs students integrated into my classes, I began to research and discover more about diversity than I would have otherwise. This allowed me to grow as a professional—and as a person who truly cares about others.

Perhaps the most exciting aspect of inclusion was the lessons learned by the rest of my students. These regular education students might never have experienced the diverse needs of people in their world until adulthood if not for the mainstreaming efforts of public education. *By actually seeing and understanding disabilities on a daily basis, your students will find ways to interact with those who are different than people they are used to encountering. They will also have opportunities to improve their RQ skills, such as empathy, communication, and adaptability.* All of your students—regular and special education—will learn to accept and appreciate each other (Jensen & Kiley, 2000).

Many years ago I taught a group of sixth graders in a large middle school. This particular group of eleven- and twelve-year-olds had mostly come from the same elementary school, so many of them knew Colin Johnston, a young man who had serious ticks that were not totally controlled by the medication he took each day. Thanks to his mother, who was a terrific advocate for her son, I received many articles related to the syndrome he suffered from as well as a fact sheet and tips for teachers. The school psychologist also stopped by before school began to give me some suggestions on working with Colin.

Once the school year started, however, I was surprised by the negative reactions and mean comments from some of Colin's classmates. I dealt with these promptly, but personally I was dismayed. How could this group of kids have been around Colin all these years and be so unsympathetic to his needs? After speaking to the psychologist, I decided to contact Colin's mom and get some ideas from her on how to best handle the situation.

To my surprise, Mrs. Johnston let me know that no other teacher had ever really talked about the syndrome in detail with the students. They had always said that Colin was "unique" or had "special needs." After a lengthy discussion, Mrs. Johnston gave me permission to cover the specific details of Colin's circumstances with the class—but she also wanted to check this out with Colin when he came home that night. The following morning I received approval from both of them, but Colin asked if he could go somewhere when I spoke to the group.

Later that morning, after Colin was sent to the library to find a fun book to read, I sat down with these sixth graders to have a heart-to-heart talk After explaining in detail about the syndrome and the fact that Colin, even with medication, could not control the grunting noises and occasional words that slipped out, his classmates seemed to appear more empathetic. Several asked specific questions, and a few even wanted to know what they could do to help Colin more. The change in my students was visible during the following weeks at school; Colin was now embraced by his classmates. Several students wanted to be his "study buddy," and one young lady even volunteered to tap him on the shoulder if his ticks started to get too loud.

This truly is what education should be all about! *If young people learn how to relate to others in more positive, empathetic ways, the world indeed will be a better place for all of us to live.* Although it isn't your job to know everything about every disability and special need, it will be your responsibility to learn about the specific requirements of the students in your class and then make the appropriate accommodations so that everyone can learn at an optimum level (Jensen & Kiley, 2000). Remember, you will not be alone in this process; your fellow professionals—psychologists, speech therapists, counselors, and special education teachers—will also be there to assist you as you adjust your curriculum, instructional methods, and classroom environment to make learning a great experience for all of these special young people.

GIFTEDNESS

As the educational system of the United States enters the twenty-first century, there has been a marked trend to identify and develop the giftedness of all children. The theory of multiple intelligences has done much to shed light on topics such as talent and ability as well as to address the adjustments that must be made in curriculum and instructional strategies (Armstrong, 1999; Gardner, 1983, 1999). However, when giftedness is discussed, this strictly refers to a select number of students "whose performance is consistently remarkable in any potentially valuable area" (Witty, 1940, p. 516). Giftedness includes the capability of performance in:

- general intellectual ability
- specific academic subject matter
- creative thinking
- productive thinking
- leadership
- visual arts
- performing arts
- psychomotor ability (Clark, 1979)

Typically, gifted children are identified well before they begin formal schooling, but certainly once they enter the educational arena they will stand out among their peers (Clark, 1979). By current definition and testing methods, 3 to 5 percent of the general population will be identified as "gifted" (Shea & Bauer, 1997). In the United States, the identification and accommodation of these special students has been interesting. Research on giftedness can be traced to at least the early twentieth century, but it was really in the late 1950s, during the Sputnik era, that politicians and educators alike became increasingly interested in the gifted and talented (National Society for the Study of Education, 1979). During the second half of the century numerous programs were implemented, including the integration of gifted students in regular education and improving specialized programs to better meet their needs (Jensen & Kiley, 2000; Smith, Polloway, Patton, & Dowdy, 2001).

Although some people may not agree with the inclusion of gifted students in the category of "special needs," it has become increasingly evident that these children do have unique capabilities and problems that must be addressed. One of the main concerns with gifted and talented students is their level of social and emotional development. In particular, self-esteem issues are often problematic; gifted children see themselves differently than others see themselves and can score lower on self-esteem evaluations than other students (Shea & Bauer, 1997). Studies have been done on the benefits on integrating gifted students into regular classroom settings so that the intense comparisons that can occur in homogeneous groups do not add to any self-concept or image problems (Jenson & Kiley, 2000; Shea & Bauer, 1997)

One of the wonderful aspects of working with gifted students, aside from their tremendous academic abilities, is that many will have a high emotional intelligence, exhibiting tremendous communication abilities. These children can interact with you on an adult level, and they enjoy discussions, debates, and dialogues both inside and outside of the classroom setting.

Another pleasant part of teaching many of these savvy communicators is that they tend to interact well with their peers, becoming wonderful cooperative learners, study buddies, and even tutors. It is important to note, however, that not all gifted students will score high in the area of RQ. In fact, some of these highly intellectual students may need assistance with relating to the regular students in the classroom. This depends upon their personality type, past relationship experiences, and exposure to other groups of students.

CLASSROOM CONUNDRUM

This year you are working with a teacher who seems to have a knack for relating to students with special needs. Not only that, but she also had several classes in special education during her master's degree program. Although you'd like to get some input from her on how to interact better with the students you share, every time you broach the subject, she seems reluctant to offer assistance. Actually, it almost appears as though she wants to keep the students all to herself. Although you hope to improve your knowledge in this area, you don't seem to be getting any assistance from your "coworker." What do you do with a teammate who really isn't helpful? Should you say something to her—or even to an administrator—about this territorial attitude? And, most importantly, how can you learn more ways to assist your students, no matter what this person does?

Refer to appendix A, "Potential Solutions for Classroom Conundrums," at the end of the book for ideas on how to answer these questions.

CHAPTER 4

Connecting with Fellow Teachers

After working for three years in private schools, I entered the staff meeting at Grant Middle School with some trepidation. I was excited to teach at a public school for the first time, but I was also intimidated by the size of the school and staff. Once again, I would be the new kid on campus—which, at twenty-five years young, I was in more ways than one. Fortunately, I had already made a great connection with my new principal, Jo Bechtold, so I knew at least one important member of my group of coworkers.

The large faculty room hummed with the happy sounds of people greeting one another after a long summer break. I caught bits and pieces of stories about travel and relaxation as I quickly made my way to the table that held beverages and doughnuts. With a glass of orange juice in hand, I stood in the back of the room and began to study the faces of my fellow teachers and staff members. That is when I spotted Mrs. Bechtold making her way back toward me. At her side was a friendly looking man with a wide grin and sparkling eyes.

"Rebecca, this is Jim Wickstrom, your new team teacher." Jo Bechtold patted me on the arm as she turned to Jim.

"Hi, Rebecca, I'm looking forward to working with you this year." Jim extended his hand, still smiling. His handshake was vigorous, and his voice seemed to bounce with energy. I liked him immediately and inwardly sighed in relief that I now knew at least one other person in my new work environment. Yet it would be over the course of the following weeks that I would really discover just how blessed I was to be partnered with this effervescent educator.

I had been assigned to teach math and science to the cadre of sixth graders that Jim and I shared. He enjoyed the language arts and social studies components—and I soon discovered that he knew how to ignite the interest of the young people in these subjects. I was amazed at the creative projects he developed, and Jim had ideas on how to improve the curriculum that I taught as well. He shared these thoughts in non-threatening ways, and he encouraged me to get involved in other activities on campus.

Perhaps the greatest lesson I learned from Jim was the compassion that he had for the children on campus—not just the ones in our classes, but all young people. He never talked down to a student, and he was always careful to get the student's side of a story. Jim went out of his way on many occasions to help students and families in need (see "Have You Seen Stephanie?" in appendix C). You could tell that he simply loved kids, so I was thrilled when he and his wife were going to have their first child at the same time I discovered I was to have my second baby.

But as often happens in education, times change and teachers move on to other assignments. After two fun-filled and exciting years of team teaching, Jim transferred to another school, and I changed to a different district closer to my home. But our story was far from over. . . .

Fast forward fifteen years. On a beautiful spring afternoon, I was standing near the baseball field at the local public high school. As my youngest son was getting ready for his first freshman game, I saw a familiar face in the crowd of parents. Jim spotted me, too, and I was immediately greeted by that wonderful grin after a decade and a half of absence. We began talking as if no time had passed between our last visit—old comrades who shared students and memories from years gone by. Apparently, Jim's son attended the same school that mine did and was also playing baseball. Our paths had crossed once more, and even though the season of life and circumstances were different, we still had much about our personal and professional journeys in common.

And, once again, I learned a valuable lesson from my friend Jim. As you are no doubt discovering, your fellow professionals can also turn out to be friends and fellow sojourners in life. They can make you better, and you can impact their lives as well. In a profession that is sometimes filled with more complaints than compliments, it is good to know that we are not alone. The connections that we make now with our colleagues are vital to our well-being—and they truly can benefit us for years to come.

BUILDING RELATIONSHIPS WITH YOUR FELLOW PROFESSIONALS

Just about every business that you can think of involves connecting with people. Even individuals who are self-employed will interact with others on a weekly, daily, and even hourly basis. The field of education is replete with these types of connections and relationships. Indeed, we wouldn't have much of a profession if it weren't for the students who go to school, the parents who make sure they get there, and the people who supply the manpower to make the whole process run smoothly! When you assume the role of teacher, you must understand that this is not a one-person show—and that is especially true when it comes to interacting with your fellow professionals.

Aside from the students themselves, your relationships with other teachers are probably the most important for you at your school campus. Why? Mostly because they are traveling down the same professional road that you are on, and they will have years of experience and expertise that can only add value to your professional life as well (Wilke, 2003; Wong & Wong, 1998). Most of your colleagues are in this helping business for a reason—and that includes improving the lives of their coworkers. So, go ahead—reach out. Ask questions. And, most importantly, listen and absorb what is shared.

One of the problems of this type of giving profession is the potential for burnout. In addition to the numerous stresses that educators face on a daily basis, this is an easy job for a person to become isolated in—especially beginning teachers who may be overwhelmed with all that they have to do and feel there is little or no time to socialize (Partin, 1999). Avoid this scenario at all costs! Even spending a few minutes a day with the teacher next door, chatting about the new reading program, the upcoming school dance, or the latest CD that tops the charts, will help you feel connected to another caring adult at some point during the day (and, by the way, you will be giving that person the opportunity to feel a little more connected as well).

There have been increased efforts in educational institutions across America to create "communities" within schools (Comer, Ben-Avie, Haynes, & Joyner, 1999; Orange, 2002). This process begins by creating on each campus a culture of collaboration that involves educators learning how to care about one another, share ideas, and work for the good of the team (Jenson & Kiley, 2000). Once such a process starts within the faculty, it can extend to the students, their parents, and the community at large. Positive interpersonal relationships are an integral part of developing a real, long-lasting sense of community and culture in any organization (Deal & Kennedy, 1982; Fullan, 1994).

MENTORING . . . AND BECOMING A MENTOR

Many school districts now offer some form of mentoring program for beginning teachers. The concept of mentoring is not new to the field of education; indeed, the practice of student teaching is all about a more experienced person guiding the "mentee" into the profession. A mentor by definition is someone with wisdom, experience, and knowledge, yet today that role has evolved well beyond an individual's days at the university preparing to attain a teaching credential (Orange, 2002).

Just because a school district does not have a specifically designed mentor program for new teachers does not mean that mentoring doesn't exist. In fact, for years more experienced teachers have voluntarily taken younger educators under their wings and guided them through the early perils of working with young people. Whether assigned or voluntary, the mentor relationship will be far more effective if it includes individuals who are not only compatible but also have similar educational belief systems (Orange, 2002). *The main focus in mentoring should be the learning relationship and the two people who are intricately involved in it* (Zachary, 2000).

The mentoring process itself should entail many aspects of inducting an educator into the profession. Helping to orient the mentee to his or her new surroundings is an initial phase of mentorship. Collaboration, or the sharing of ideas and concepts about teaching, is another way the mentor and mentee can work together. Encouragement is a key aspect of developing stronger professional and personal interactions (Sweeny, 1990). Whether short or long term, the mentor's goal should be to focus on a learner-centered relationship where the needs of the mentee establish the guidelines for the process. Then, as the connection between the two develops, more accountability and responsibility can be shared (Orange, 2002).

Despite the time and effort involved, a mentor receives substantial dividends from his or her role. Here are a few of the positive aspects about the mentoring process for the professionals involved:

- Educators have the opportunity to give back to the profession some of what has been given to them.
- Mentoring allows teachers to spend time reflecting—something that they might not be able to do in their normal, everyday routine.
- Mentors gain fresh insights about their jobs as they watch other educators in action.
- Assisting others in a professional setting develops better EQ (emotional quotient) skills that extend into one's personal life as well.

Some of these educators report that the mentoring of teachers, colleagues, students, friends, and relatives from other racial and cultural groups has allowed them to be more self-reflective about their own identity as well as to become more multicultural in their outlook (Howard, 1999). "If we are to be effective and sustained in our efforts, White educators must be immersed in a co-responsible community of support with a richly diverse group of peers, mentors, and allies" (Howard, 1999, p. 117).

If your school or district does not have a formal mentoring program, you can certainly take it upon yourself to find an older, wiser colleague who will be happy to spend time with you. You might discuss how your classes are going, ask questions about the culture of your work environment, or perhaps address specific behavior concerns. Making this type of connection will be vital for your professional growth, but it will also allow you to form a relationship that may indeed last beyond the first few years in the classroom.

LEADERSHIP IN SCHOOLS

When we hear the term *leadership*, particularly in education, our thoughts tend to automatically run toward superintendents, principals,

MULTICULTURAL MATTERS

Specific cultural activities not only allow your students to expand their personal awareness, but they also provide opportunities for them to dialogue with others and begin to create a shared "classroom culture." The following assignment can be used in most educational settings, and it will address both "objective culture" (artifacts, food, clothing) as well as "subjective culture" (attitudes, values, beliefs).

Personal Coat of Arms

Please design your own coat of arms that will represent who you are and what things you believe in. Using colored markers or pencils, draw at least one picture that represents how you feel about each of the following categories:

- Family
- Favorite holiday or food
- Your most outstanding quality
- Hope or dream for the future

and department chairpersons. However, in today's diverse school settings, this is only part of the educational picture. *While these leaders by definition play key roles in the operation of schools and school districts, it is the everyday classroom teacher who is often overlooked as the cornerstone of day-to-day leadership.* In fact, the perception of teachers among students, parents, and community members often defines their views of educational leadership (we will discuss the administration further in chapter 5).

As Wong and Wong (1998) explain, "There are two kinds of people: Workers and Leaders. . . . [W]orkers are preoccupied with time for breaks, holidays, overtime, and work hours" (p. 271). Leaders, by contrast, have a professional approach to their careers. They are concerned about enhancement, cooperation, achievement, and efficiency. Teachers are educators who lead both inside and outside of the classroom setting, but it is up to each individual to decide to take up the mantle of leadership in this profession (Wong & Wong, 1998; Jensen & Kiley, 2000).

For many experienced teachers, it is particularly difficult to acknowledge the term *leader* as part of their résumé. One study found that fewer than 10 percent of classroom teachers defined themselves as "teacher-leaders" (Vance, 1991). This may be due in part to decades of subliminal induction by educational institutions across this country. In other words, teachers were taught that they were employees who worked in classrooms under the guidance and direction of the administration at both the site and district level. The classroom was their domain, but anything beyond that would require the "expertise" of those who specialized in leadership.

Fortunately, we've come a long way from these narrow views about the skills and abilities of teachers. Indeed, a study done in the 1980s identified classroom teachers as the real leaders in education due to their own knowledge and experiences as well as their day-to-day decision-making abilities (Jensen & Kiley, 2000). *Today's diverse classrooms require teachers who are scholars, policy and decision makers, advocates, and activists in education* (Kincheloe, 2004).

As you begin to consider your role as a leader within this profession, realize that what you say and do has tremendous impact on everyone who crosses your path. First, your students are looking to you for leadership—and they are quietly assessing and integrating the skills that you impart to them. In addition, the students, their parents, and your colleagues will follow your example when it comes to the greater circle of leadership around you. In other words, even if the administration at your school is weak or struggles in some areas, your support of those leaders can be contagious. Rather than bickering about bad decisions around the water cooler, you can choose to be supportive, while actively addressing needs and working toward positive changes. Getting involved in making improvements on campus is much more productive than complaining, and proactive steps such as this will define just what kind of leader you are as well.

As you have probably already deduced, good interactions with others are at the heart of sound leadership; "leaders must be consummate relationship builders with diverse people and groups—especially with people different than themselves. Effective leaders constantly foster purposeful interaction" (Fullan, 2001, p. 5). The teacher-leaders of the twenty-first century must improve their relationship skills in addition to fostering great connections with those around them. This is especially true as we strive to create inclusive classroom environments where all learners can interact and learn at the optimum level (Odden, 1995; Henze, Katz, Norte, Sather, & Walker, 2002).

DEALING WITH DIFFICULT COWORKERS

Perhaps one of the most challenging aspects of any job is interacting with individuals who chose to be negative, unpleasant, and even downright obnoxious. Within the confines of any company, whether small or large, there is the potential to have employees who struggle with interpersonal skills—or, even worse, seem to sabotage attempts to build positive, productive relationships with their coworkers. Although this type of scenario is rarely discussed during the preservice learning experience, every seasoned teacher can vouch for its reality.

What can you do when you encounter a colleague who is, to put it as kindly as possible, difficult to deal with? The first step to take is one of personal responsibility (Wong & Wong, 1998). *Despite how this individual has chosen to act, you have the choice to remain professional.* If he or she speaks to you in a discourteous fashion, reply as pleasantly as possible, and move on to the responsibilities you have to your students and your school. Don't take on their problems as your own—and don't try to fix them. You have a job to do, so stay focused.

But this doesn't mean that you have to bear any demeaning comments, insults, crude language, or harassment. Report anything that truly seems professionally inappropriate to an administrator on campus. You may want to schedule a private meeting with the principal to discuss this problem and get suggestions on how to handle it better. More than likely, the individual involved already has a reputation for this type of behavior; if so, any incidents must be officially documented as the administration attempts to deal with this challenging employee.

Being aware of potential problems that you may confront on your campus is vital to your success as a professional. As many experts have noted, the stresses of today's educational experience are partly why teachers leave the field of education—particularly in the first few years of their career (Odden, 1995; Jensen & Kiley, 2000). To increase retention rates, educators must be prepared for potential dilemmas, which sometimes includes dealing with conflict in a positive, proactive manner. (Further discussion on how to address these types of concerns with other staff members, parents, and community members may be found in chapters 5–7.)

Learning some simple techniques to address various conflicts can also aid in sidestepping or solving problems early on, before they grow out of proportion. Some ideas on how to manage potential conflicts when they arise include:

- Don't avoid people or situations just because they are difficult.
- Create an open environment where everyone feels free to share differing perspectives.
- Affirm each and every perspective. Involve everyone in the process.
- Discuss options for resolution together, attempting to find a common ideal that everyone can agree upon (Goleman, Boyatzis, & McKee, 2002).
- Once the conflict is aired and the resolution is agreed upon, redirect everyone's efforts toward getting things back on track.

By taking personal responsibility for how you react to a given situation, you are also showing leadership. For example, you might divert a coworker from constantly being negative about things that occur on campus because you try to maintain a positive attitude about the work environment. Perhaps you intervene in a conflict by asking a penetrating question that will allow that person to think about a situation more intently. *While you cannot—and should not—avoid people simply because they tend to put a damper on the day, you certainly can set an example of what an exceptional educator is all about.*

THE ART OF REACHING OUT

As you have considered the concepts in this chapter about developing better connections with your colleagues, hopefully you have been able to personally reflect on your own experiences in relating to others. If not, spend a few minutes now thinking about the relationships that you have been in over the years—both personally and professionally. What strengths have you seen within yourself that benefited those interactions in a positive way? Are there areas that you would like to improve upon so that future interactions will be more productive? If so, what are they, and how can you take proactive steps toward improving your own RQ?

For some people, reaching out and relating is as natural as drinking water. These individuals have the innate ability to perceive other's feelings and communicate their own in an interesting, engaging manner so that friends, family members, and even new acquaintances understand them as well. This is that emotional quotient or interpersonal intelligence that was discussed earlier (Armstrong, 1999; Gardner, 1999; Goleman, 1995). *For those who are gifted in other intelligences, the good news is that one's ability to relate can be improved upon with very specific activities and experiences* (Armstrong, 1999; Gardner, 1999; Jenson, 1998).

One of the best ways to enhance your relationship techniques is to learn all that you can about the topic. When it is to interpersonal and relational skills, this means starting with a simple game plan. On a sheet of paper, draw a line down the middle. On one half, write what skills you already have that allow you to communicate and connect well with others; on the other half, list those areas that you struggle with. For each of these shortcomings, do a little research to see if there is a book, a tape, or even a class that you can take to help you address these specific needs. Finally, target only one area at a time that you want to improve upon; otherwise you will be overwhelmed before you even get started.

For example, if one of your areas of weakness involves speaking in front of your peers (believe it or not, this is not uncommon for teachers), then perhaps a group such as Toastmasters would be a perfect solution. Maybe you have a hard time making new friends; then you may want to find a nonintimidating activity such as a community class, book club, or service organization to join.

A few of the following simple suggestions for interacting with others may also immediately improve your communication abilities:

- Face the person that you are talking with and look him or her directly in the eye as you speak.
- Keep your body posture open; in other words, don't cross your arms (a sign of insecurity or nonopenness).
- Ask a question or two about him or her. This shows that you care about who you are speaking to—as an individual as well as a coworker.
- Ask clarifying questions or attempt to summarize what the person has said.
- If you forget details, make notes about these interactions in a journal so you can refresh your memory from time to time about issues that are important to your friends and colleagues.
- When you cross paths with these individuals again, ask specific questions about the things they have shared with you.
- Drop by another teacher's room just to say hello; see if he or she needs anything as you head to the copy machine or office (Armstrong, 1999; Jenson, 1998).

As you fine tune your interpersonal relationships with your fellow teachers, be prepared for some amazing results. Not only will you feel more connected on your campus, but you will also begin to build the confidence that you need to improve the interactions that you have with others in your life. You will learn all sorts of surprising things from your colleagues—from tips on curriculum to insights about classroom management. Plus, your coworkers' diverse backgrounds, cultural nuances, and wide array of experiences will open your eyes to a far bigger world than the four walls of your classroom. Don't be afraid to expand your horizons—you may be pleasantly surprised at how you can positively impact the lives of others in your world too!

CLASSROOM CONUNDRUM

Over coffee one afternoon, a fellow teacher shares about some interpersonal problems she's been having on campus. At first, you are taken by surprise because Jessica has always been an outgoing, self-confident young woman who reaches out to others on a regular basis.

But this is exactly part of her dilemma. Her strong interpersonal skills have actually been a turnoff for some staff members. After Jessica shares a few examples, it becomes apparent that a few of these individuals are envious of her obvious ease with people. Others might be overwhelmed by her effervescence. How can you help her out? What advice can you offer Jessica to improve her connections with others, even though she really rates highly in most RQ areas?

Refer to appendix A, "Potential Solutions for Classroom Conundrums," at the end of the book for ideas on how to answer these questions.

CHAPTER 5

Connecting with Your Administration

I finally received the phone call I had been waiting for all summer, although it was now August and the new school year was quickly approaching. As difficult as it would be to leave the school I had worked for, I was eager to be closer to my children and not have as long a commute to and from work. My principal had personally contacted her former colleague and recommended me for a rare opening in this popular public school district.

The new school's secretary seemed friendly, and she efficiently informed me about the particulars of the job interview, which was only days away. I began preparing the file I usually took with me to interviews and contemplating questions I might be asked. When the big day arrived, I walked toward the glass doors that led to the main office with some trepidation. A receptionist smiled at me from behind her desk, which reassured me that this might be a great place to work after all.

This woman directed me toward the back of the administrative office complex, where I found an equally kind face—the principal's secretary, with whom I had spoken several days earlier. I relaxed more when she directed me to take a seat in a nearby chair and said that Kathryn McKinley, the principal, would soon call me in for the interview. As I watched the second hand tick around the large wall clock, I breathed deeply and whispered a silent prayer. Before long, a door opened and out stepped a tall woman in a tailored skirt and matching blazer.

"Hello, I'm Kathryn McKinley. You must be Rebecca. Welcome, and please join us in the conference room."

There was no time for small talk; Mrs. McKinley turned and rapidly strode through the door. I had to double my steps to keep up with her. Six people were chatting around a large oak table, but they stopped their conversations as the principal entered. She pointed to an empty chair and then swiftly slid into her own at the other end of the room.

Underneath that table my knees began to knock. Never before had I been part of a team interview process. This group consisted of the two assistant principals, one of the school counselors, the department chair, and two other teachers. Thirty minutes later, I left the room exhausted. A battery of questions had been presented to me, and I had done my best to answer each one. My final assignment before leaving that day was to complete a short essay on my philosophy of behavior management.

Although I looked for some positive sign of approval on the faces of my interviewers, especially from the principal, I couldn't detect anything definitive. In fact, Mrs. McKinley sat stoically in her chair, making notes on a large yellow tablet. On the drive home, I replayed the interview over and over in my mind; the only conclusion that I could arrive at was my uncertainty as to whether or not Mrs. McKinley liked me at all.

To my surprise, the following morning I received a personal call from Mrs. McKinley asking me to join her staff! Her tone was extremely pleasant, and she spent fifteen minutes going over the details of the first teacher workdays, which would begin in two weeks. At the time I could hardly believe the transformation in her attitude, but I eventually discovered that this complex leader had many interesting sides to her personality. Sometimes she appeared to be strictly concerned about the business operations of the school, yet Mrs. McKinley also cared about her staff and wanted to develop close ties with everyone on campus. She had a passion for the field of education, and she took her chosen profession very seriously.

LEADERSHIP BEGINS AT THE TOP

By nature of their job description, principals are school managers and administrators (Fiore & Curtin, 1997). They are also now, by virtue of the school reform process taking place across the United States, considered to be "change agents" (Fullan, 1994, 2001). Although leadership within the educational setting certainly does not begin or end in the front office, the principal must set the tone for leadership, enforce the district directives and state mandates, and ultimately, take responsibility for the overall management of the school site.

In a survey done in the late 1980s and early 1990s, it was determined that there were approximately eighty thousand public school principals and twenty-five thousand private school administrators in the United States (Fiore & Curtin, 1997). Within this large body of educators were dedicated professionals who listed improving literacy skills and encouraging academic excellence among their chief career goals (Fiore & Curtin, 1997). An interviewing process done by Stanford University (2000) noted that many principals are eager to improve their skills in order to enhance reform efforts, and they appreciate the transformation of their role into "instructional leaders."

Perhaps not so surprising is the fact that the majority of public school administrators were still male—59 percent in large urban schools and 75 percent in small town and rural settings. In the nation's public schools, 84 percent were also white, non-Hispanics who made an average of $54,800 per year. In private schools, women represented the majority, but again, these school administrators were mostly white, non-Hispanics, and their average salary was only $32,000. Interestingly, the average age of principals in all school settings was forty-five to forty-eight years (Fiore & Curtin, 1997).

Many of these school leaders work their way to the top by beginning as a classroom teacher. After additional education and experience, and after attaining the appropriate credentials, they choose to assume this pivotal role, although this often happens by starting as an assistant principal to gain more leadership experience. This type of hands-on learning allows administrators to relate better to the teaching staff on their campus, and it also prepares them for their continuing position as teacher/leader (Fullan, 1994). *The goal for principals of the twenty-first century is to help design the learning process in such a way that the people under them can deal successfully with critical issues as well as work on their own professional development* (Fullan, 1994, 2001; Odden, 1995).

As a teacher, it is important that you understand the key role that your principal plays in running your school campus as well as being an advocate for both students and staff members. You will need to have a good working relationship with this individual because he or she is the person that your school district has hired to supervise you and your school site. When there are problems or concerns, your principal is a resource for you—especially on issues that are serious and require intervention. This includes issues with difficult students, challenging parents, and even conflicts with colleagues. The bottom line is that the buck stops at the principal's desk (Wilke, 2003).

Everyone hopes to have good leadership at corporate headquarters, and this is no less true in educational institutions. However, just as there are deficiencies within business organizations, some school administrators have their shortcomings. Most educators would agree that the leadership role of the principal is pivotal, and when these administrators are perceived to be weak or inept by the staff, their ability to lead and direct the learning process decreases (Fullan, 2001). *While you cannot control the ability level of your principal, you do have the choice to follow and do the best job you possibly can, both inside and outside of the classroom.*

Fortunately, you will discover that many of the school principals that you encounter will be outstanding leaders who want to make a difference in the field of education. They are caring and compassionate, and most importantly, they are driven to make your school community a more successful place where all students can learn and live up to their potential. Get to know your principal; glean all that you can from him or her. Even if mistakes are made, these struggles can challenge you to improve yourself both personally and professionally.

Principals Really Can Be Pals

As I mentioned earlier, my initial experience with Kathryn McKinley made me uncertain about her. Within twenty-four hours, once I was able to see another side of her personality, those feelings changed. Isn't this the case with some people who you come in contact with on a daily basis? First impressions or gut responses are often totally unfounded; once you truly get to know individuals, you discover that there is more to them than originally perceived.

This is a vital piece of information for you to tuck away in your RQ tool kit. *It takes time to develop relationships—and this is especially true with those who have a supervisory role to play in your life!* The principal has a duty to perform, and as much as he or she may also wish to relate to you on a more personal level, this position will always influence your relationship. Over the years, after many interactions, discussions, and experiences together, Mrs. McKinley and I grew closer as professionals. While we never became best friends, a mutual respect and rapport developed that made our daily encounters much more meaningful and enjoyable.

The emphasis on building better relationships within corporate and educational settings is at the heart of reform (Fullan, 2001; Jenson, 1998). As Fullan (2001) summarizes, "schools and school districts can get tough about student learning, can use their minds to identify new and better ideas, . . . but successful strategies always involve relationships, relationships, relationships" (p. 70).

While it is true that one of your principal's duties is to assist you in handling problems with students, parents, or colleagues, you should work on building a rapport with this leader long before a serious conflict or dilemma arises (Wong & Wong, 1998; Jensen & Kiley, 2000; Weinstein, 1996). For example, as the new the school year approaches, you can meet with your principal to discuss what the schoolwide discipline plan is and verify that your classroom management program fits into its guidelines (Wong & Wong, 1998). You should also check in with him or her periodically when you have questions that require more expertise than you can get from other staff members. Your principal will probably have a scheduled visit or two to your classroom, but why not invite him or her in to observe on a day when the students have something special planned?

In addition to providing practical solutions to everyday problems, your principal can also help you develop as an educator. Some of the best advice that I ever received about professional growth came from assistant principals, principals, and superintendents. These leaders had already traveled along the educational road that I was just beginning, and they were aware of many of the opportunities both inside and outside of the district. They shared ideas about classes, seminars, and workshops to attend as well as what advanced degrees would be beneficial to me as I expanded my career goals.

Speaking of professional assistance, many administrators are also well-connected within the educational community itself. Your principal may move on to another school where you'd like to work someday; perhaps he or she has a friend that could be a connection for a future job. The administration is also typically informed about many of the professional organizations that educators can join to enhance their knowledge and expertise. By developing a relationship with your school leaders, you will not only grow personally, but you will also gain a whole new appreciation for your profession.

THE DISTRICT OFFICE CONNECTION

The "big picture" of leadership within any school district initiates at the central, or district, office. If we use the analogy of a solar system, the district office would be similar to the sun, with the schools orbiting around as satellites—separate entities, yet under the control of the larger, central body. For each school district, this central office comprises an administrative staff that oversees curriculum and its implementation, financial matters, personnel concerns, and a variety of programs and policies that impact the schools under its supervision (Spring, 2002).

The chief executive officer of any district is the superintendent. During the late nineteenth century the role of superintendent was primarily fiscal in its origins, but this position evolved and expanded with the developing public school system (Odden, 1995). By the second half of the twentieth century, superintendents were not only creating the vision and direction for school districts, but they were also serving as managers and intermediaries at both the local and state levels (Odden, 1995; Spring, 2002).

Perhaps it is this transformation in focus that caused many staff members to feel more and more distant from the superintendent as well as other leaders at the district level. Many educators interact with the personnel department and possibly a few administrators at the district level when they are initially hired, but once they begin working at their school site, additional contact is often minimal. Fortunately, the reform efforts of the late twentieth and early twenty-first centuries have encouraged decentralization at the district level and fostered the concept that the leadership should intentionally work on building better relationships with their schools and staff members (Fullan, 1994, 2001; Spring, 2002).

MULTICULTURAL MATTERS

Many school sites are attempting to improve multicultural awareness and connectedness on campus. Try the following activity with your students, and then mention it to an administrator as a possible project for the faculty. You can even suggest that some of your students run the human scavenger hunt activity described below at an upcoming staff meeting!

Human Scavenger Hunt

During the next ten minutes, find at least one person for each of the items listed below. Once you have filled up all of the spaces, take your seat and prepare to share what you have learned about the other people in the room!

1. Birthday in the same month as mine: _____

2. Born in the same state that I was: _____

3. Same color eyes: _____

4. Likes the same style of music I do: _____

5. Is fluent in a second language: _____

6. Owns a dog, cat, or other pet: _____

7. Enjoys a similar book, movie, or computer game as I do: _____
   _____

8. Traveled to a country outside the U.S.: _____

9. Plays or likes to watch the same sporting activity I do: _____
   _____

10. Loves the same kind of food or restaurant as I do: _____
    _____

As a professional educator, it is essential that you know who the members of your district's leadership team are. Even if you have little contact with them, you should be aware of the names of people who are in charge of key departments, and hopefully you can start to connect faces with these names as time goes by. The superintendent and assistant superintendents tend to visit every school periodically, and they could show up in your room unexpectedly. This has happened on numerous occasions during the course of my K–12 experience.

While interacting with student teachers on a variety of campuses, I have been encouraged by the hands-on approach of many of today's district leaders. At one large public school, I discovered the superintendent visiting for the entire day—and this occurred again later in the semester. On one of these visits, I noticed him talking with parents in the main office as well as guiding a substitute teacher to her assigned classroom. It may be that this superintendent had learned the value of building positive relationships and was putting his skills into action!

While some teachers are wary of the "movers and shakers" at the district level, you need to realize that they are simply people like yourself—and they are trying to make a difference for young people, too. And many of them are more than willing to assist their colleagues if they would only take the time to ask. Hopefully, you will get to know these important colleagues over the course of the next few years, especially as you attend workshops, seminars, and school board meetings. In addition, talk to your principal about becoming involved in districtwide committees. Not only is this an opportunity to become familiar with other educators in your district, but it is also an excellent chance to grow as a professional (Wilke, 2003).

LEARNING TO CONNECT WITH LEADERS

Throughout this book, you have seen that building relationships is an art—and a skill that you develop over time. Some individuals have an easier time than others, but for most people, learning to connect with leaders is a difficult task. Why? Often this is due to feelings of intimidation involved in the process of relating to those in leadership. No matter how nice or friendly an administrator may be, or how approachable he or she may seem, you know that inevitably this person has the power to hire and fire—and that includes you!

The very role of leadership impacts the way that people relate— and it should. There must be a respect factor involved between employee and employer. There should also be a politer, more formal interaction—at least initially—between the head of the corporation and those who support the business. In schools, teachers don't chat and bond with their assistant principal, principal, or superintendent as they would with a coworker, school secretary, or member of the custodial staff.

Another aspect that is often overlooked is that some leaders truly struggle with their relationship quotient. Despite the fact that they have worked their way up through the ranks of educational institutions, these administrators, who score high when it comes to IQ, may fall short when it comes to connecting with their colleagues. Perhaps this is why there are so many books on leadership development today, as well as increased efforts to assist leaders in learning how to improve their emotional quotient (Fullan, 2001; Lencioni, 2002; Jenson, 1998; Blanchard, Zigarmi, & Zigarmi, 1985).

Whatever your administrators' RQ levels may be, there are steps that you can take to improve communication and interactions with them. It is helpful to be aware of your own principal's method of leading. *There are essentially four leadership styles, although there can be various behavioral nuances within these categories. They are directing, coaching, supporting, and delegating* (Blanchard, Zigarmi, & Zigarmi, 1985). For example, your administrator may be the type of leader who gives specific instructions and monitors these tasks to see that they are completed. This would be a direct style of leadership. If your principal prefers to facilitate efforts on campus and encourages others to make the necessary steps to fulfill them, she has more of a supportive style.

Some teachers I know are hesitant to interact with their administrators on a more in-depth, personal level because of previous bad experiences—even dating back to when they were in school. Yet as a professional, you must realize that connecting with the leaders on your campus is not only crucial for your current success, but it is also vital to your future professional life. If you encounter someone who is more difficult to relate to, there are specific steps you can take to open up the lines of communication. These include (Jenson, 1998):

Think before you talk. Make sure you say what you mean to communicate.

Listen. Be sure that you try to hear what the other person is saying.

Put the speaker at ease. Watch your body language, facial expressions, or other visual signs that may make the person you are talking with uncomfortable.

Don't be afraid of conflict. "The absence of conflict can be a sign of decay" (Fullan, 2001).

Keep an eye on the emotional barometer. Remember, this isn't all about you!

Don't get distracted. Avoid doodling on paper, looking at someone else who is walking by, and so forth. Keep your focus on the other person.

Give communication some time. Don't watch the clock or rush off to do something else until this interaction is finished.

Ask questions—and more questions. This clarification process will help ensure that you truly understand what the other person has said and vice versa.

As I learned with Mrs. McKinley, understanding leaders takes time and effort. I did develop a deeper working relationship with her, and she also became a mentor for me in my professional life. As you strive toward building better relationships with your administrators, remember that these leaders are a unique group of people. They have not simply risen to the top; they have taken specific steps and overcome many obstacles to get there.

School administrators also must fulfill specific directives that include ensuring that all children are learning, maintaining an environment that is safe for students and staff, and verifying that everything done in the district falls within federal, state, and local guidelines—and, oh yes, making certain that the annual budget is not exceeded! It is a demanding, often underappreciated job. As you improve your relationships with the administrators at your school and within your district, you will also be able to learn a great deal about how to communicate more effectively with other executives, pacesetters, and key players in the world around you.

CLASSROOM CONUNDRUM

A former colleague of yours, Bob Finley, calls one night for your advice on a situation that's developed at his new site. Evidently, the principal who hired him really likes Bob and always asks him to work on various committees and projects. The problem is that this principal has not always treated the staff respectfully or fairly, so over the years he has developed some enemies. The division among the staff has created a work environment that is at times unpleasant, especially with the constant grumbling by some disgruntled teachers. But now negative comments are being directed at Bob; some of his coworkers feel that he is being disloyal to them by helping the principal. One of them even suggested that he should say no whenever the principal asks him to join another committee. So far Bob has been able to avoid any direct confrontation, but he knows that he must say something. Should he talk to his principal? Can he continue assisting in these extracurricular assignments and still remain on good terms with his other colleagues?

Refer to appendix A, "Potential Solutions for Classroom Conundrums," at the end of the book for ideas on how to answer these questions.

CHAPTER 6

Connecting with Parents

Lin Quan grinned while her father stood in front of the room full with sixty-plus students. I had noticed her glowing smile the first day of school when I correctly pronounced her name (which doesn't always happen, but I was certainly rewarded for my effort this time). A few weeks later, at back-to-school night, I met Mr. Quan, who was reading the volunteer sign-up sheet I had posted on the door. In slightly broken English, he asked me what the "guest speaker" section was all about. I explained that we encouraged parents to come in and share stories about their experiences, college choices, professions, or other areas of life that might be beneficial to the students.

Then Mr. Quan grinned—and I definitely noticed the family resemblance. He asked if he could come in one day to share the story of his family's escape from Vietnam. My heart skipped a beat. "Of course," I promptly replied, "it would be a wonderful opportunity for all of us." As a teacher who promoted multicultural education, this was exactly the type of real-life story that I felt would truly benefit students. Little did I know that my own life would be changed because of this family's tragic yet triumphant tale.

On this particular Friday morning in late October, Lin's father was the second guest speaker so far that semester. As the students settled down in their seats, Mr. Quan began the story that started when Lin was only eighteen months old. He explained about the Communist takeover of his country and of the danger his family was in because of their previous political connections. He knew that he had to escape with his wife and five children, and the only way would be to travel out to sea. One night, their chance came. Over one hundred people crammed aboard a small boat and set out for the ocean, hoping that no one would spot them. Unfortunately, a lone soldier along the riverbank heard some of the children crying and opened fire. Several people were hit, including Lin! Although the wounds were not fatal, there was no one on board to perform the medical procedures needed to help those who were injured; they would have to wait to get help.

As dawn approached, these refugees found themselves drifting far from their homeland. In a humble manner, Mr. Quan explained how the adults on board elected him to be captain of their vessel because of his past sailing experience. Days passed, and he did what he could to keep the people calm and working together. Finally, a U.S. Navy vessel approached and rescued them from their cramped quarters. The ship took these weary passengers to the nearest refugee camp, where they began the long process of immigrating to America.

Mr. Quan concluded his talk while the audience of eleven- and twelve-year-olds sat transfixed. The girls next to Lin hugged her. I looked over at my colleague, who like me, dabbed at the tears in her eyes with a handful of Kleenex. This is what we had been trying to teach our students about American history—it is the land of the free and home of the brave—and before us were two examples of those brave, free people who make up this amazing country. And, after a simple twenty-minute talk by this parent who chose to share his story, the students understood more than they could have if they'd read about it in a book.

Like my students, I had also learned an invaluable lesson, but mine was one that I had least expected. That day I finally grasped the concept that each student comes to my class with rich life experiences. I also realized how essential each parent is to the educational experience. My eyes—as well as my heart—were opened to a fuller understanding of my students and the importance of their families.

ANOTHER PIECE OF THE EDUCATIONAL PUZZLE

Most educators would agree that the parental role is essential to the development of a healthy, well-adjusted child. Indeed, research reveals that individuals develop 50 percent of their intelligence from conception to age four (Bloom, 1964). In fact, Benjamin Bloom also concluded that because of the vast amount of development that takes place in the early years of life, school and home environments should be mutually reinforcing for optimum learning to take place.

Since the beginnings of the educational system in America, parents have been a big part of the educational picture. When the Massachusetts General Court passed the Old Deluder Satan Act in 1647, it required that every town of fifty or more families hire a reading and writing teacher in order to educate the children (Ornstein & Levine, 2000). Because of the linguistic and cultural diversity of the Middle Atlantic colonies, many churches there established parochial schools to meet the needs of the local families. During this colonial period, the population in the South was widely dispersed, but wealthier families were able to hire private tutors or to send their children to boarding schools in towns such as Williamsburg or Charleston. Unfortunately, poorer southern families suffered because of the lack of educational opportunities (Ornstein & Levine, 2000).

From these early American parents to present-day caregivers, there has been a strong sense of concern about and commitment to the education of young people. However, in more recent times, *the process* of educating children has seemed to take a more prominent role than *the parental involvement* both behind and within school settings. It is not as if parents have taken a back seat in regard to educating children, but rather it often appears that educational institutions have sent them to the last row in the auditorium. They have become almost an afterthought in many minds—far behind the curriculum, standards, goals, instructional methods, accountability, grade-level requirements, test scores, budget concerns, and so on.

Does this strike you as true for your school site too? If you're not sure, take a look at the agenda for your next staff meeting. What parental concerns will be addressed? As in many educational settings, there is a strong possibility that this meeting will be filled with the needs of the district, county, or state rather than those of the families that make up your community.

How about outreach to parents and guardians? Other than back-to-school night and parent conferences, what does your school do to involve the students' caregivers in the day-to-day learning experiences? If you can list more than letting them volunteer or hosting a spring concert, then yours is doing better than most campuses. Yet how many times have you sat in the lunch or faculty room and listened to laments about uninvolved parents? Could there be other reasons for their unexplained absence on your campus?

Although educators may not want to hear this about their profession, these topics must be addressed if teachers, administrators, and support staff truly want to help all students survive and thrive in today's school communities. There are certainly many complex reasons for the change in connectedness between homes and schools since the early days of American history, but the current issue for educators is what can be done to make school sites real communities where caregivers feel welcome.

What can you do to enhance the relationships with these key players in the process of educating young people? Do you value their involvement in the students' lives? Do you make attempts to call, write notes, say hello in the halls, and even invite them in to visit or become involved in your classroom? What steps would you like to take to improve your connections with parents, guardians, and caregivers? Let's spend some time contemplating how you can enhance your relationship skills with the ones who love, protect, nourish, clothe, and educate your students the other ten hours of their waking day.

INVOLVING PARENTS IN TODAY'S SCHOOLS

Perhaps the place to begin building better relationships with the primary caregivers of students is evaluating your view of these essential members of the educational process. For instance, if you were to remove the title "parent" or "guardian" and replace it with "first and foremost teacher," how would your interactions with them change? Certainly, there might be more initial respect as educators look upon these individuals as fellow professionals—colleagues on the home front.

Interestingly, this concept about parents has been part of social reform movements since the seventeenth century (Jensen & Kiley, 2000). In fact, a translated work from the eighteenth and nineteenth centuries expresses that "for children, the teaching of their parents will always be the core, and the role of the teacher is to provide a decent shell around the core" (Gordon & Gordon, 1951, p. 26). In more recent times, researchers have studied various approaches to creating a school community that includes families in the educational process. This creative approach to teaching today's diverse student population and preparing them for the global world in which they live *necessitates* parental involvement (Comer, Ben-Avie, Haynes, & Joyner, 1999; Cole, 1995; Schaps, 2003).

It makes a tremendous amount of sense for parents to be involved in their children's schools, and the benefits of their input, support, and physical presence are tremendous. Some of these include:

- Students who attend schools with a strong sense of community are more likely to be motivated to perform, and they tend to behave better both inside and outside of the educational setting (Schaps, 2003).
- Parents and teachers working together convey expectations to children that influence achievement (Wong & Wong, 1998).
- Involvement of caregivers in learning activities at home can assist in developing the social and personal skills of children (Cole, 1995).

In addition to shifting the paradigm of the role of the parent from simply provider to one of "first and foremost teacher," those involved in the field of education must take the initiative to include these caregivers in the learning process. In other words, it is up to administrators, teachers, and support staff to find the common ground between families and schools. This means analyzing the parents' expectations for education as well as the expectations that schools and districts have of them. Mutual concerns include student academic success, giving and receiving respect, effective communication, and the creation of caring, comfortable learning environments for children (Jensen & Kiley, 2000).

If your school or district doesn't take time to discuss these kinds of issues, then as a classroom teacher, you can certainly address them yourself. Once you begin working on forming positive connections with parents, guardians, and caregivers, you should start to see these improved relationships benefit your students both inside and outside of the school setting. You may even decide that this transformational process is important enough to share with your fellow teachers and administrators. Perhaps your efforts in this area will increase your colleagues' understanding of why it is essential to include these key people in the business of educating children.

Finally, teachers need to realize that there are many different styles of parental involvement. Some caregivers feel that by volunteering one day out of the year, they have fulfilled their obligations to the school. For others, sending money for a fundraiser is how they show that they care about kids. A few parents will be at your classroom door the first day of school (or even before), asking how they can help out each week.

There are also varying types of involvement between grade levels. Many parents and guardians seem to be ready and willing to assist at the elementary school level, but this often tapers off during the middle school years and can drop drastically in high school (Wilke, 2003). A possible explanation for this decline is that parents have been slowly trained over the years that their assistance is not needed within the domain of the educational institution, particularly as the students get older. For example, in the primary grades, caregivers are personally asked to serve as drivers on field trips or to bake cookies for parties, but by the time their kids enter middle and high school, they begin to receive generic "volunteer slips" from a formal parent group. No wonder there is often an abundance of parental participation in elementary schools and a small cadre of parents who are brave enough to venture on to high school campuses!

Fortunately, culture can and does change. As an educator, you can ensure that your classroom is welcoming for every person who enters—and that includes the caregivers of your students. Help all parents feel "invited" to participate in your program rather than "dis-invited" (Wong & Wong, 1998). Here are some simple suggestions to get you started:

- Make a personal phone call to each and every home during the first few weeks of school, even if it is only to leave a voice message to introduce yourself and let the caregivers know you'll be in touch.
- Send home notes to the parents and guardians so that, by the end of the first month of the new semester, every family has received a nice message about their student.
- Post a volunteer list on your door so that parents can see how they can be of assistance to you and the students.
- Create a monthly newsletter with highlights of the class activities—including parent volunteers who helped out.
- Host a special event each quarter where parents can simply visit and see the students in action.

Although thinking about ways to get your students' caregivers more involved in the educational process will take some time on your part, the rewards down the road will far outweigh any extra pressure you may feel by adding this to your current agenda. Enlisting the efforts of these core educators now will also aid you in building better connections with the kids in your classroom.

WHAT TO DO ABOUT OVERINVOLVED PARENTS

Although many teachers wish that more parents and guardians were involved in the educational experience, there are some cases where caregivers can be overinvolved. One of the strangest cases of overinvolvement happened to a colleague named Carol. At the end of one school day, Carol stopped by to ask if I needed anything, since she was headed to the workroom. "No," I replied, thanking her for the thoughtfulness; then I started to erase my chalkboards. I was only halfway done with one board when I heard the sound of high-heeled shoes clicking rapidly down the concrete pathway in front of my classroom. As I turned to look in that direction, Carol frantically burst into the room.

"Can I hide in here?" she asked breathlessly.

"What's happened? Carol, is everything okay?" I was truly worried when I noticed the desperate look on her face.

"It's Mrs. Grantham again. She's been here every day after school asking about how her son is doing, and she stays to talk at least thirty minutes! If I leave early, she calls me at home. I know Blaine is her last child at home, and she's very overprotective, but I just can't take this any more!"

I quickly closed my classroom door so that Mrs. Grantham wouldn't catch my friend on the verge of tears. We were barely into the new school year, and this middle school mother had driven her son's teacher to a near breakdown! As Carol divulged more of the story, it became obvious that this mom simply couldn't let go of her growing boy. She was clinging to him by trying to stay too involved in his educational (and no doubt other) experiences. Something needed to be done for everyone's sanity.

Fortunately, a savvy administrator soon intervened and included a school counselor in the initial meeting with mother, teacher, and son. The process of helping this mother gently let go of her adolescent so she didn't smoother him—and his teacher—wasn't an easy one. In fact, it took

MULTICULTURAL MATTERS

Parents and guardians are vital links between home and school. Getting these caregivers more involved in today's classrooms takes some time and energy, but the impact on the entire school community will be invaluable. Below are a few ideas that have been successful on campuses around the country. Why not implement some of them at your school or even start a unique multicultural movement of your own!

Newsworthy: Start a classroom newsletter in two or more languages. For editing and production purposes, enlist the assistance of parents who speak different languages. Make sure the students help with these journalistic efforts as well.

Guest speakers: If your school has a volunteer program, find out what parents, guardians, or other caregivers are available to speak to your students. They may be able to talk about their visits to other countries, their career choices, or even their own cultural interests. Let the parents of your students know that you want to start a guest speaker program, so they can become more involved in your classroom.

Cultural celebrations: Celebrations in classrooms and on school campuses can reflect the unique aspects of the community's culture. How about starting a multicultural fair at your school site? And, while you're at it, why not include other cultures in addition to those of the school community so that students, parents, and staff can increase their knowledge and appreciation of the world around them?

---

several weeks of work to establish and stick to good boundaries. Mrs. Grantham was asked to stop by only one afternoon a week, and she promised to call the school, not Carol's home, to leave messages. Carol also improved her own communication skills with all her parents, especially learning how to wrap up meetings and unexpected drop-in sessions in a timely manner. Blaine got in on the act by sharing more about what was going on at school with his mother so that she didn't feel left in the dark.

The overinvolved parent is often the least expected type of parent in an educational setting. Many teachers have been trained to prepare for the opposite end of the spectrum: parents who are too busy, or even parents who don't appear to care about how their kids are performing academically. Perhaps the easiest way to understand all of these dynamics is to realize that there are many parenting styles as well as ways that your students' families operate. Today's educators must be aware of these variations as well as how to intercede in situations when needed (Jensen & Kiley, 2000).

A question that many teachers ask at this point is when does the involvement of a parent become *over*involvement? The scenarios will vary, but the answer to this is relatively simple: *a caregiver is too involved when the normal learning experience for the child is becoming affected in a negative way by the parent's or guardian's actions.*

The story about Mrs. Grantham provides a perfect example. Caring about how her son was doing at school was not the problem, but being at the classroom door in the afternoon—every afternoon—was excessive. Talking to the teacher in detail about the day's events and her son's progress crossed the line of what is normal interest and concern. Another signal was that Blaine had become so embarrassed about his mother's daily presence that he had begun to run from the class as soon as the bell rang.

There are a few overinvolved parents who aren't always observed at school; instead their handiwork will be seen—literally—by the teacher as he or she grades papers and projects. These are the caregivers who not only decide to help James and Jessica with their homework, but who also feel obligated to do most of it for them. While their intentions may be good, they overstep the boundary discussed earlier: the normal learning experience of the child is affected in a negative way when they, not the children, do the work!

Many excuses given by these well-meaning folk have been heard by educators at every grade level all across America. Some parents say that they simply want their children to get more sleep, so they help them finish writing a paper. Others insist that a certain project was too hard for their kids, so they decided they'd better do it. When asked why they didn't bring this concern to the teacher weeks ago when the project was assigned, these overzealous caregivers usually shrug their shoulders and express that it seemed easier to just take care of matters on their own. For educators, these types of situations on a rare occasion are not so worrisome; many parents have had to assist a child with finishing an assignment or wrapping up a project. *The "once in a great while" intervention is not the main concern; rather it is the routine assistance of the overinvolved parent.*

What can you do when you cross paths with this type of parent of guardian? Certainly don't run away from the problem as my friend Carol did; instead, you should face the dilemma head on. You should never avoid a relationship that needs work, but do take time to analyze it, devise a plan of action, and then try your plan with the person(s) involved. Since your primary goal as an educator is to allow your students every chance to succeed, you need to have healthy interactions with their caregivers.

Part of the problem with overinvolved caregivers is that they have established poor boundaries when it comes to the lives of their children. The reasons for this are complex. Perhaps they are controlling people by nature, or they might be filling some emotional void. These parents may even be acting out of guilt (Cloud & Townsend, 1992).

Although it isn't your job to teach healthy boundaries to parents, you can start by establishing good boundaries in your own professional life. For instance, at the beginning of the school year, you should make parents aware of when you will be available to talk and where they can reach you. In addition to school phone numbers, some teachers feel comfortable providing caregivers with home numbers and e-mail addresses. Once again, it is up to you to establish the guidelines for the use of contact information. Are there certain hours you want to be available? Do you want to set a time limit on personal calls?

When it becomes apparent, as in the case of Carol and Mrs. Grantham, that some other means of intervention is necessary, don't hesitate to talk to an administrator about your concerns. Sometimes he or she will have further ideas on how to address the situation. In fact, this administrator may have already had previous encounters with the caregiver. This also gives the administration a heads up to a potential problem that may need further action in the future. Most importantly, don't wait to ask for assistance until you are frustrated or the circumstances are out of control. These issues are best addressed early so that everyone involved can have a successful school year.

WHAT TO DO ABOUT ABSENTEE PARENTS

While it is essential in many professions to assume the best of others, this is especially true for educators when it involves working with students, parents, and coworkers. This means keeping a positive attitude toward some of the most difficult parents and guardians—those who are technically AWOL, or absent without leave. In other words, these are the type of people who have either abdicated their role as caregiver or reluctantly retain it with minimal energy and effort.

Next to abuse, this emotional abandonment is almost impossible to understand or excuse, yet it is all too often a reality that teachers must deal with when working in today's classrooms. As sad a situation as this is, twenty-first-century educators must accept the fact that "schools are the only community institution that must receive and educate every child within their boundaries: every learning, physically, and emotionally disabled child; everyone who is abused, neglected, undernourished, or without guidance; every substance-abusing child; and any child who was affected in-utero by a drug-using mother" (Mendler, 2001, pp. 4–5). *Education is about helping every young person achieve and succeed in life—no matter what type of home or family he or she may come from.*

As you consider ways to better assist your students who have a parent or parents who are uninterested or uninvolved in their lives, it will be worth taking some time to contemplate why situations occur. According to the U.S Bureau of the Census (1992), there has been a steady increase in the number of adults and children who reside in single-parent, blended, or other households. This study also reported that only about 10 percent of all households in America could be considered a "traditional family," that is, one that includes two or three children, a stay-at-home mom, and a father who works.

Due to many of the changes in modern society, parents and caregivers often must make adjustments in order to provide for their families, or even help them survive. For example, single parents must work in order to provide food, clothing, and other material needs for their children, thereby reducing the amount of time that they might have for extra activities, such as being involved at the local school. Some children are raised in foster homes or by grandparents. According to a 1996 report by the Census Bureau, 2.14 million children were living in homes where no parent was present and another relative served as the head of household (Jensen & Kiley, 2000). Unemployment or struggling to make ends meet also impacts how much caregivers are involved in the students' educational experience.

And these situations are just the tip of the iceberg when it comes to analyzing the reasons a parent is—or appears to be—an absentee parent. As an educator, you will not be able to spend time lamenting over these unfortunate scenarios; your energy will be better used in determining how you, the teacher, can make adjustments in order to assist these young people in achieving at the optimum level this school year.

One of the first clues about an absentee parent will be the lack of response to your calls or written messages. This individual will not be at back-to-school night, and usually he or she will be a no-show at the parent conference. You might also identify them because the student will often be prepared and have a wide array of excuses for why papers are not coming back from home, why none of your phone messages have been returned, and why his or her caregiver is never seen at school. Despite these signs of abandonment, you must do your part by following through. Don't stop calling, but be sure that you document the messages you have left or the attempts you've made to contact the parent or guardian.

If essential papers are not being returned promptly—or at all—it may be time to take this matter a step further. You may need to speak to the school counselor or an administrator about the family. These colleagues may have additional insights into the situation, especially if they have dealt with these individuals before. They may also be able to intercede and make progress in retrieving some of the vital communications needed from home. It may be necessary to set up a meeting between you, the caregiver, the school counselor, and an administrator.

Some of these interventions may work immediately, and other problems with AWOL individuals will be resolved eventually. Unfortunately, other cases may take much more time and effort to work out. During my years of teaching in both public and private schools, I had one or more experiences per year with absentee "caregivers" who tended to be a challenge all year long. What should you do in these situations? The answer is simple—you continue to do what is best for the child!

As frustrating as these absentee parents and guardians can be, the student in your class still deserves to learn, to be nurtured, and to grow and develop into the best person possible. Rather than become frustrated with these problematic individuals, focus all the energy that you can muster on helping the student in unique ways that will empower him or her.

Be sure to stay personally connected with these children on a daily basis—in part because if their parents are negligent in school matters, they are probably not as involved at home as they should be. Try to discover any special interest that these kids have so that you can provide books, passes to the computer lab or library, or even times to play games with peers. You might also want to talk to other teachers and staff members to apprise them of the situation and enlist their help in giving extra attention to these kids whenever possible.

Although nothing can replace the real presence of a parent, your role as teacher will be invaluable to these young people, who need your support, encouragement, and follow-through when primary caregivers either cannot or will not offer theirs. Not only will you be building relationships that will make a difference now, but you will also be setting an example for these students as they step out into the world and make connections on their own.

WHEN HOME PROBLEMS INTERFERE WITH LEARNING

As we discussed above, there are a variety of reasons that caregivers may be absent from the educational experience—both on campus and at home. This scenario alone can cause problems that impact how students feel about school. If parents don't set high expectations for their children, they often won't understand why they should try to achieve academically (Wong & Wong, 1998). Because of their own disinterest in reading, writing, and the acquisition of knowledge, parents can automatically instill a lackluster approach to learning.

But there are other real-life problems that impact student achievement; poverty, hunger, and homelessness are just a few of the serious issues facing young people today. The Children's Defense Fund (1998) reports that kids who live in poverty are more likely to drop out of school than their peers. Although many schools provide subsidized lunches, millions of poor children are not served breakfast or offered summer food service programs. Research done in 1994 discovered that families with young people represented approximately 39 percent of the homeless population (Jensen & Kiley, 2000).

While these larger social issues may seem daunting to educators, your awareness that some students may be experiencing these types of circumstances will allow you to take steps on their behalf. For example, you can investigate what programs are available at your school or within your district to help students get materials and supplies that their families may not be able to afford. You can also ensure that those students who should receive subsidized food have all the information necessary to become enrolled in these programs. Once young peoples' needs are identified, you will have the chance to alert other key staff members who are involved in their educational experience and enlist their assistance as well.

There are other egregious problems that greatly impact the lives of today's youth. Substance abuse, violence, and child abuse, neglect, and endangerment are concerns that teachers must be cognizant of in school communities. Whether the substance abuse is found to be a parental problem or perhaps the young person is beginning to experiment, everything from simple concentration in class to behavioral problems can result. Be on the lookout for unusual signs or symptoms that your students may convey—and don't hesitate to report these concerns. Each state also mandates that school personnel and child-care workers report suspected child abuse or neglect. Even if you are uncertain whether or not something qualifies as abuse, discuss the situation with an administrator who can offer a second opinion.

The bottom line is that although educators are not only the providers of knowledge in learning environments, they are also a type of "insurance agent." This means that all members of the school community must make every effort to ensure that students are safe and able to learn. If there are home problems that seem to be interfering with a child's participation in school, then it is your responsibility to assess the situation, develop an action plan, and make every effort possible to assist the student to get back on track.

BRIDGING THE GAP WITH NON–ENGLISH SPEAKING PARENTS

Diversity within the population has greatly increased in many regions of the United States. This demographic expansion provides today's youth with an amazing opportunity to interact with people from many language and cultural backgrounds that they might otherwise have to travel around the globe to experience. Despite the numerous benefits that these multicultural changes in our communities offer, there are also some realistic concerns that educators must address.

One important factor that is of prime concern for school communities is the interaction with parents and guardians who speak little or no English. While this may seem daunting to staff members, consider what these caregivers must be experiencing. Many are living and working in a new country, and are attempting to do so while acquiring a different language. Can you imagine if you were asked to teach in Italy or Japan next week—and, by the way, you get to learn the language as you go? This kind of situation would be overwhelming to most adults, particularly when they desire to communicate properly because it involves the care of their children (Jensen & Kiley, 2000).

Since many non–English speaking parents may feel intimidated or embarrassed when they interact with school personnel, it's up to the educators involved to reach out and bridge any language gaps that may exist. Fortunately, there are numerous educational institutions across this country making tremendous strides toward improving communication for all members of the community. Most of these districts and schools have responded so promptly because they recognize that, for students to be successful, educators must understand and engage their culture, home language, and learning style (Garcia, 2002). Not only must the child's language be acknowledged and valued, but it should also be implemented in the school environment (Garcia, 2002; Freeman & Freeman, 1998; Nieto, 2000). And, equally important, the parents of these children must become part of the educational process.

In the diverse student population of one elementary school in southern California, over forty language groups are represented. In order to better meet the needs of the families of these students, parent volunteers have been organized to translate materials into most of these languages. Although it took time to implement this cooperative effort, now caregivers can know what is happening at their children's school.

Another school district, with a relatively small population of second-language learners, decided that it was essential to provide English classes for parents in order to aid them in understanding school procedures, educational forms, and student homework. There has been such a positive response from the community that many of these parents and guardians now encourage their friends to take the free courses. Other towns have responded to the needs of newcomers to their communities by offering translator services or classes that can be taken in order to improve their English skills.

As a busy teacher who is trying to meet all of the demands of your students on a daily basis, you may not feel that you have the time to reach out to non–English speaking parents. While you should keep your focus on the kids in your class, you must also realize that their parents and guardians play an integral role in who they are and who they will become. The more you are able to build positive connections with these caregivers, the more likely it will be that you'll have their support and assistance when you need it most. Even the smallest effort to reach out can reap great rewards. There may already be services in place within your school, district, and community that can assist you in this process. Keep your eyes and ears open, but mostly be ready to engage all of your students' caregivers positively whenever the opportunity arises.

CLASSROOM CONUNDRUM

During a parent conference, it becomes obvious that the caregivers involved are struggling with how to help their child, who is not performing well at school. Currently Gabriella has a D in math and seems to be more interested in her softball team than in learning. One of the parents looks at you and says, "We're simply out of ideas on how to get Gabriella motivated. She's the youngest of four children, and we're worn out and tired of the whole schooling thing. What would you do if she were your child?" How do you respond to this parent? What kind of advice can you—or should you—offer?

Refer to appendix A, "Potential Solutions for Classroom Conundrums," at the end of the book for ideas on how to answer these questions.

CHAPTER 7

Connections with Other Key Players in and around Your School

When Jackie Jansen offered to come in and talk to my students about the history of quilting, I was thrilled that this seasoned seamstress wanted to interact with my multicultural band of middle-schoolers. The 5'2" sixty-some-years-young lady appeared energetic enough to keep the adolescents' attention for at least thirty minutes, and her expertise would add just the right touch before the group embarked on the final project I had planned. As this petite senior citizen awaited my decision, I couldn't help but wonder why she was so excited about spending some of her free time with teenagers.

It didn't take me long to figure out the answer to that question. From the moment Mrs. Jansen entered the classroom, my students seemed as interested in her bubbly personality and sparkling blue eyes as I had been. She almost bounced to the front of the room, as though she was only thirteen years old. Hanging off her arm was a large canvas bag that overflowed with brightly colored fabrics. She held it protectively, as if these items were precious treasures that she might be gracious enough to share if we earned her trust. My normally boisterous class turned and twisted in their chairs to get a better view of her, silencing one another with whispers, all eyes in Mrs. Jansen's direction.

I watched the lesson unfold from the back of the room with a mixture of awe and amazement. Mrs. Jansen wove a tale about the history of quilting from around the world that in and of itself was a priceless tapestry. Within ten minutes she had taken the students from ancient Africa to medieval Europe, talking about the types of fabrics utilized and sharing stories that were told in the quilting process. When she reached the quilt makers of American colonial days, she pulled the hand-stitched log cabin design from her bag and explained how her great-grandmother had made this out of the scraps of old clothes and bedding.

The students gasped at the sight of the ancient treasure, then raised their hands to ask Mrs. Jansen questions. I could not believe this was the same group of kids that had moaned only a week earlier when I had embarked upon this topic as a means of integrating history, cultural heritage, and art into my curriculum. But the best part of Mrs. Jansen's lesson was yet to come.

"Would you boys and girls like to have a chance to make a quilt yourselves?" she asked, her eyes twinkling as she scanned the classroom. I noticed that she carefully avoided looking my direction.

"Yes!" the students shouted in resounding harmony. That's when she sheepishly smiled at me.

"Well, Mrs. Wilke and I will have to talk and see if we can work it out, but I know some of my fellow quilters would *love* to help you make a classroom quilt."

At first, I was not sure how to respond. Usually we were lucky if we got a volunteer to come and speak to *one* class, but now I had someone who wanted to return for what would have to be at least several visits. And her idea was far superior to my concluding activity, which entailed merely drawing their own quilt pattern from some library books I had collected.

After I introduced the day's math lesson to my students, I spoke briefly to Mrs. Jansen about her plans. She had the fabric, the scissors, the thread—everything we would need to aid the students in planning, measuring, designing, cutting, and yes, even sewing a quilt square of their own. She had already spoken with her quilting friends, and they were as eager as she was to become involved with these middle school students. It seemed that they had a mission to pass on the art of quilting to the next generation. "Okay," I replied, "let's give it a try."

I must admit that the next few weeks had a few glitches—for example, rearranging the curriculum so that I could fit this fascinating learning experience into an already packed schedule was challenging. Yet during those busy days, I realized what rich lessons my students were acquiring; and they were also utilizing mathematical skills as well as kinesthetic learning. I did have to adjust my classroom organization—

and expectations of organization—especially when the corners of my room soon had stacks of fabric samples and quilt batting and there were scraps of every color fabric strewn across the carpeting. The students, however, did not notice the mess—they were too excited about this class project. And, before the month was over we had a beautiful, multicolored and multicultural quilt hanging on our wall!

As always, I think that I may have been the one who gleaned the most out of the entire experience. Once again I realized the power that an interesting person can have with students and the curriculum. In addition, I had never really utilized the volunteer program at my school, but I would do so faithfully—and in other subject areas—in the years to come. The benefit of building relationships with people outside my usual circle of coworkers and colleagues was definitely reinforced. Mrs. Jansen not only refreshed my memory of how to use a needle and thread, but she also showed me the beautiful tapestry that can be made in life when diverse patterns—and people—join together in unique, unexpected ways!

SEEKING SUPPORT FROM THE SUPPORT STAFF

One of the missing pieces in some university courses for preservice teachers is imparting an understanding of how to fully utilize all of the team members available in the education process. Schools of education strive to prepare new professionals so that they are knowledgeable in their subject areas, confident in their instructional techniques, cognizant of the latest concepts in classroom management, and aware of the current state guidelines, frameworks, and standards (Darling-Hammond, Wise, & Klein, 1999). Anyone who has worked on a public or private school campus, however, can confirm that there is literally an entire community of people actively involved in educating young hearts and minds.

In addition to the teaching and administrative staff on every campus, there is another large cadre called "paraprofessionals" who allow the school to run well and help ensure the overall success of students. *These members of what is often called the "support staff" do just that—they support the roles that the credentialed faculty and administrative team members must fill day in and day out.* Paraprofessionals include the school secretary (or secretaries on larger campuses), custodians, food-service providers, bus drivers, security team members, and paraeducators such as teacher aides (National Education Association, 2004).

The relationships that you build with your coworkers not only enhance your efforts as an educator, but they also result in your feeling more satisfied and complete as a person (Wong & Wong, 1998). Some of the most integral relationships that you can form early in your career will be with members of the support staff. From the first day that you walk on campus, these key people can help you with everything from locating the supply room to learning how to order materials for your students. In *The First Days of Class*, I mentioned that one of the first paraprofessionals that I made friends with was the custodian (Wilke, 2003). Why? Because this individual always knew where everything was—and if he didn't, he certainly could find out quickly. When a sink overflowed in a science room I taught in, who do you think came to the rescue? That's right—the ever-faithful custodial staff!

According the National Education Association's website (2004), there are approximately 350,000 Education Support Professional members in the NEA organization alone. On average, these K–12 employees have nearly eleven years of experience working with educators. They also make up over 40 percent of the total K–12 workforce. Do you think that the type of expertise they possess will be useful to you as you attempt to provide students with the optimum experience each day on your school campus?

Although they are trained and ready to provide assistance, remember that support personnel are probably not going to track you down and ask what kind of aid you need. They have their own job descriptions and functions that they must fulfill. If you appear to be "handling things" (even though you might very well be overwhelmed in the process), they will assume that you are doing just fine and will move on to assist others who are asking questions or expressing specific needs. In other words, these essential players in the education process are there to be of assistance, but they aren't mind-readers. You must let them know what you require so that they can provide it for you.

For new teachers, this is not always an easy task. Sometimes there is a fear of appearing as though you are not prepared or knowledgeable about how schools function. Please toss that notion out the window.

Support staff members realize that the recent arrivals on campus are the ones who really can use assistance, and they want to offer that now so that you won't need as much guidance down the road when other employees join the team. Becoming familiar with these people can start simply by perusing your school's personnel directory or by asking a seasoned colleague about these paraprofessionals.

In addition, you may be fortunate enough to be assigned a paraprofessional or educational assistant (sometimes called "teacher's aide") to work directly with you and the students. These cooperative situations can be difficult for some educators, especially if they haven't been trained how to best utilize these individuals within a classroom setting. First, never make assumptions about this person's training or experiences with children (Lindberg & Swick, 2002). Second, get acquainted with him or her by asking informal questions, and be certain to strategize together to develop a schedule and plan for working in your class. Next you may want to ask an administrator about the specific job description for this paraprofessional. Also, be sure to deal with any disagreements or tensions immediately, but never in the presence of the students. As time goes by, you will find that by forming good connections with educational assistants, both you and your students will reap the benefits of having their added expertise in your classroom.

Try to interact with all of the support staff that you come in contact with in a friendly, professional manner. Take time to chat for a few minutes in the workroom or at the copy machine. Start up a conversation with the custodian before you ask for something. And, by all means, follow up with a verbal thank you or send a personal note of appreciation when someone goes out of his or her way to assist you. As you begin developing these vital relationships with support staff members, be sure to share about yourself as well. They will be just as interested in knowing about you since you're now part of the school community.

VOLUNTEERS ON TODAY'S SCHOOL CAMPUSES

The concept of volunteering on school campuses is not a new one by any means, but the popularity of this charitable contribution of time, effort, and energy has definitely increased over the past several decades. Some of the emphasis on volunteerism in today's public schools can be credited to the Goals 2000: Educate America Act passed in 1994. This piece of legislation was due in part to the 1983 report *A Nation At Risk*, which revealed declining scores and lack of standards for America's schoolchildren (Jensen & Kiley, 2000).

By encouraging efforts to raise standards nationwide, to improve the availability of technology to classrooms, and to set high expectations for students, teachers, and parents, Goals 2000 also enhances partnerships between schools and their community members. This cooperative effort should include educators, parents, businesspeople, and other community members for the purpose of providing every child with a world-class education (U.S. Department of Education, 1996). Even though the majority of volunteers on any given campus are usually the parents of the student body, there are other individuals, from relatives to caring community members, who also assist in elementary, middle, and high school settings (Jensen & Kiley, 2000).

The leadership team should develop a clear plan for any volunteer program as well as the procedures needed for attaining these types of services (Henze, Katz, Norte, Sather, & Walker, 2002). For example, there must be a well-established system for interviewing and placement of all volunteers. Specific guidelines and expectations should be agreed upon by everyone involved in the process (Jensen & Kiley, 2000). The staff needs to look for individuals who have the typical traits necessary to work well with young people; these traits include helpfulness, sincerity, creativity, dependability, reliability, confidentiality, and responsibility (Rasinkski, 1995).

Before seeking volunteers for your classroom, ask the following questions to be certain that you need extra assistance:

- Are there times in the day when I could use an extra set of hands to perform basic tasks such as cutting, gluing, stapling, copying, or filing?
- Could some of my students benefit by working one on one with another adult?
- Would I be able to facilitate additional small-group activities if I had someone helping out in my room?
- Could the curriculum be enhanced by the addition of guest speakers or special projects?

- Would I plan more field trips or community events if I had more parents volunteering during the school year?

People who like to interact with students usually know their areas of strength, and they will more than likely share those with you before they begin working in your class. I experienced this over a decade ago when a parent, who also happened to be a talented artist, offered to teach watercolor techniques to my group of sixth graders. She was eager to impart some of her knowledge as well as purchase the paint and brushes if the school could supply the special watercolor paper. Needless to say, I found money in the budget and quickly accepted her offer.

Soon my students had the chance to enjoy several sessions of painting under her supervision. When additional art funding became available later in the year, I called this helpful volunteer to see if she would like to assist in some different types of art experiences, such as ceramics or painting with acrylics. In her usual polite manner, she declined, stating that watercolor was her area of expertise.

Some volunteers will not be this specific. In fact, many individuals will simply express their interest in helping kids, and then they will assume that you will find specific tasks for them. And there are plenty of ways that they can fit into most school settings! In elementary school, they can read to students, help out in small-group activities, or attend field trips. At the secondary level, volunteers might share information about their careers, teach a lesson on a foreign language or different country, or work with students one on one (Jensen & Kiley, 2000).

As an educator, you will be responsible for overseeing their efforts— so be sure that you have a predesigned plan before they enter your class. This avoids having to stop a lecture with your students to give directions to the adults who cycle in and out throughout the day. You may even want to set up a volunteer station in the back of the classroom where these individuals can go and look at notes you've prepared for them about what needs to be done.

Whether volunteers work directly with students or behind the scenes preparing materials, organizing activities, and sorting supplies, the collaborative partnership that you form with them will be an enormous advantage to your students. In the fast-paced, curriculum-rich classrooms of today's schools, teachers are blessed to have an extra pair of hands

MULTICULTURAL MATTERS

Why not invite parents and members of the community to your school for a multicultural tea? The students can assist by researching various types of tea from around the world as well as goodies that can be bought or prepared easily. During this event, present your ideas about including these valuable members of the community in school activities throughout the entire year!

You are cordially invited to our first annual multicultural tea!

When:

Where:

Why: So we can get to know you better!

What to expect: Our students will be serving teas and goodies from around the world to you, your neighbors, and fellow community members. Be ready for special music, entertainment, and lots of fun!

and eyes in their classrooms. While some educators may hesitate to incorporate volunteers because they are afraid of the extra time and effort it initially takes to get them organized, eventually these partnerships will pay off exponentially. Not only can volunteers become resources for you and your students, but they also add to the diverse cultural environment that you are developing in your school community.

CONNECTIONS WITH THE BUSINESS COMMUNITY

In the early days of American education, the formation of public schools rested in the hands of parents and politicians (Spring, 2002). This is not to say that the business world did not have an interest in how the youth were educated, for indeed many of those involved in the establishment of educational institutions focused on the social and economic needs of the developing nation. Besides reading, writing, and arithmetic, our founding fathers realized that schools must adequately prepare its citizens for their future (Spring, 2002).

During the twentieth century, the investment of corporate America in education increased at a rapid rate. This seemed to be a natural development, especially due to the growing global economy; as technology and travel improved, there was a demand for a different kind of workforce. Leaders in the business world looked to the nation's public schools to help provide competent, flexible employees. By the 1990s, the National Governors' Association also encouraged parents, business, and community organizations to work together in the advancement of educational programs (Spring, 2002).

The Goals 2000: Educate America Act passed in 1994 also clearly urged the partnership between educators, community members, and businesses (U.S. Department of Education, 1996). One of its directives was for school districts to develop rigorous occupational skill standards in order to "define the knowledge and skills needed for complex, high-wage jobs" (Jensen & Kiley, 2000, p. 436). Few people questioned the rationale that students should be more prepared to enter the workforce—and they seemed comfortable with the interest of the corporate world in the required changes.

Corporate America's involvement in public schools is a profitable venture in many ways. When businesses get involved in the development of curriculum, the setting of standards, the implementation of technology, and even the training of teachers and students, the chances of acquiring workers who are prepared to fill potential positions increase. The employees of any given company also have an opportunity to reach out and serve in their community as volunteers. Some companies can also employ students as apprentices in on-the-job training programs (Comer, Ben-Avie, Haynes, & Joyner, 1999).

The involvement of business in education offers many advantages to schools as well, especially when there are economic downswings and cutbacks. Companies that are in "adopt-a-school" programs often supply equipment, materials, guest speakers, consultation for curriculum, professional development for staff, and even money to their assigned educational institutions (Comer, Ben-Avie, Haynes, & Joyner, 1999). As Fullan (2001) explains, the future of "knowledge societies" depends upon educators and business leadership cooperating more than ever before. Even though some concern has been raised about the possible influence that the business world can gain through monetary or material support, the trend of corporate America being linked with local schools seems unlikely to be reversed in the twenty-first century (Spring, 2002).

As a classroom teacher, you should investigate what companies may already be helping your school site. If none are currently involved, then talk with your principal about looking into this type of sponsorship. One of the easiest ways to find a company that may want to get involved with students is to contact the local chamber of commerce (Comer, Ben-Avie, Haynes, & Joyner, 1999). Many businesses like to give to local schools, but they often wait until they are approached and apprised of the specific needs. There may be instructional materials available to you as well as people who want to serve as mentors or tutors. And, as you reach out and get more involved in the community, you will discover that the contacts you make in the business world will be extremely beneficial to both you and your students.

MAKING A REAL COMMUNITY

There is no doubt that relationships are an integral component of education, and a primary objective for teachers is to be able to relate to their students. Once you connect with the young people in your class in a personal, caring manner, you'll be better able to help them achieve to their potential. The next part of this important process involves building good connections with the students' parents as well as your colleagues. By doing so, you will develop the support system that you need as a professional so that you will not simply survive your job, but you will also thrive in every aspect of your career!

Your interactions with others in the school community are just like the proverbial pebble thrown into the quiet pond: the students receive the initial burst of energy, and then parents, coworkers, and other key people in the educational community are affected as you spread your sphere of influence. *Then, and only then, will you have the opportunity to motivate and engage others who should be part of the educational puzzle—those members of the community who want to be connected to you and your students.*

Because of the dynamic changes in today's society, many experts in the field of education believe that the community must play an important role in the reform process in education (Comer, Ben-Avie, Haynes, & Joyner, 1999; Comer, Haynes, Joyner, & Ben-Avie, 1996; Garcia, 2002). There are a variety of programs within many communities that can benefit school sites as well as the students and parents. For example, there may be "community health, cultural, recreational, and social support" available through various organizations (Garcia, 2002, p. 160).

Throughout America, community service groups, universities, and government agencies are providing tangible support to local schools in order to improve the educational opportunities for all students (Comer, Ben-Avie, Haynes, & Joyner, 1999). An independent, nationwide organization called Communities in Schools (CIS) serves over 1,500 school sites by connecting them with numerous resources to help improve the quality of instruction and experiences for young people (Orange, 2002).

As members of the community are welcomed into the educational "circle of friends," rapport is built and trust is formed. These neighbors and business people are able to see firsthand the tremendous efforts being made on behalf of the students, and often they are encouraged to increase their own support for the next generation of citizens. When educators reach out to others outside of the school site, their campus becomes a more "functional community" (Comer, Ben-Avie, Haynes, & Joyner, 1999).

One of your most crucial roles is to create a sense of the community for your students (Keefe & Jenkins, 1997). What better way for children to experience what a wonderful place the world can be than to see you, their parents, their neighbors, and members of the community involved in their lives—both inside and outside of the classroom? And, as relationships are formed and strengthened between students, parents, staff, and members of the community, young people get to experience "a fully functioning prototype of the healthy, just society in which we hope all our children will spend their adult lives" (Comer, Ben-Avie, Haynes, & Joyner, 1999, p. 51).

THE ART OF GIVING BACK IN RELATIONSHIPS

A lesson that I learned from Mrs. Jansen and her team of quilters is that life affords us many chances to give back to others. These ladies took time out of their schedules to connect with the students in their community when they could have chosen to do something else. They enjoyed every minute of the crazy days in our classroom, and the kids flourished amidst the fabric and fascinating historical tales of quilt making.

As an educator, when you connect with the key players in your professional life, you too will have multiple opportunities to hone the skill of giving back. At first the relationships may seem somewhat one-sided—after all, when you ask a support staff member for assistance, he or she may seem like the only one providing a service. Yet take a step back and look at the interaction in the bigger picture. True, you may have asked that the custodian bring a stack of construction paper for your art lesson, but this request alone allows you to make a personal connection. Were you smiling when you spoke to him or her? Did you take time to converse a bit and try to brighten his or her day?

In addition, when the custodian does deliver the paper, you'll have the chance to show your appreciation. You can have the students say hello and thank him or her for taking time to help out. These small gestures of politeness and communication are fundamental to forming a relationship with this staff member. The custodian will also begin to know who you are; plus, he or she may really like to have a break from the bathrooms or lunch area to actually interact with teachers and students. And, of course, as the students observe you connecting with others, they'll have a hands-on example of what "relationship" and community are really all about!

Besides the steps that you take at our own school site to include support staff, volunteers, and members of the community in the interactions of today's diverse classrooms, you will also have the chance to get your students engaged in the world around them. Learning about community events and service has been part of citizenship education in the United States since public schools themselves were formed (Weah, Simmons, & Hall, 2000; Ovando & McLaren, 2000).

Many school districts now require that students interact with the community in order to graduate from high school. In Chicago during the late 1990s, the nation's third largest school system expected students to perform forty hours of some type of outreach in order to receive their diplomas. One reason for this type of program is to help young people to gain a sense of community. As one official put it, "They need to know that community is about giving, not just getting" (Spring, 2002).

There are many wonderful examples of students reaching out into communities across America. In New York, young people from the Yonkers Public Schools invited government officials and merchants to an economic summit—and they made certain that the forum was conducted in English, Spanish, and Arabic so that everyone could be involved and comprehend this activity. The government actually learned from this student-run event and began offering translation capabilities in their own forums (Comer, Ben-Avie, Haynes, & Joyner, 1999).

At Joshua Tree Intermediate School, the staff and students wanted to build better relationships with the neighboring Native American community. They constructed a pathway between the school and the neighborhood—one lined with native plants that had cultural meaning—so that everyone could commute back and forth to meetings and events much more easily. Plus the students learned lessons about how each plant had a story and meaning to the Native Americans (Henze, Katz, Norte, Sather, & Walker, 2002).

Cultural awareness as well as attributes of RQ are some of the lessons that all members of the community naturally acquire as they begin to connect with one another. Indeed, service to others is an integral part of many communities of color (Weah, Simmons, & Hall, 2000). As the twenty-first century unfolds, educational institutions across this nation are discovering that the diverse classrooms of today and tomorrow must also learn how to look beyond themselves and reach out to the world around them. "It has been, quite properly, the role of the public schools, the *common schools*, to nurture a sense of community—one that binds us together while respecting differences" (Ovando & McLaren, 2000, p. 70).

This leads us back to you—the educator who actually interacts in schools and classrooms on a daily basis. As you continue to improve your own RQ, you will discover that reaching out to those around you will become increasingly easier. *The small strides you make toward communicating, cooperating, and connecting with the key players in and around your school will pay tremendous dividends down the road.* Start with simply getting to know more about these important people, and then look for ways that you can reach out to them. Try to encourage these individuals to engage in the educational process; you will be amazed by the impact of these powerful connections as a real community forms around you and your students!

CLASSROOM CONUNDRUM

As you interact with people on your campus, you notice that one individual has been particularly unfriendly. Despite your best efforts, this support staff member doesn't respond in a nice manner—and sometimes she won't complete the tasks you request. Although you could probably avoid her most of the time, there are some instances when you must go through her in order to get various items of school business accomplished. Although she's frustrated you to the point of anger at times, you know this type of response isn't professional—and it can also be highly unproductive. What can you do? Will it seem as though you are tattling if you talk to an administrator? Are there other interventions you should try first in order to resolve this uncomfortable situation?

Refer to appendix A, "Potential Solutions for Classroom Conundrums," at the end of the book for ideas on how to answer these questions.

CHAPTER 8

Welcome to Our Global Future

After years of studying Spanish, I was excited to travel to the Central American country of Costa Rica. The pictures I'd seen had been enchanting—quaint buildings, ancient cathedrals, and mysterious rainforests. Although my stay would be short, I planned to visit schools in the capital of San Jose and interact with as many people as possible. This would be one of my first cultural experiences outside of the United States, so my mind raced with many questions.

The friends who met me at the airport drove me around the city and gave me as much information as they could about the places that I should see during my visit. The following day, I was introduced to their *ayudante*, Maria, a Costa Rican who was assigned by the language school to assist my friends. After some discussion, I discovered that this was a typical procedure for language acquisition in this country. The *ayudante*—which literally translates as "helper"—offers assistance not only in learning Spanish but also in adjusting to the new culture.

I thought this was an amazing concept, and I asked how many people would need an *ayudante* in Costa Rica? Weren't most of the inhabitants Spanish speakers?

"Oh no," Maria replied, "We have numerous people who come to our country from all over the world. Why there are over thirty thousand U.S. citizens alone who have retired and come to live in Costa Rica!"

Another day during my trip included a stop at a local elementary school where I was quickly surrounded by dozens of children who wanted to talk to "the lady from America." They spoke so rapidly that my head started to swim; but gradually I sorted out the words and began to answer their questions. They were curious about what the children did in my country, what kind of games they played, and what their schools were like. Then some of the kids wanted to take me to their classroom to show me a project that they had just finished. When their teacher nodded her assent, I followed them into the large, two-story building that housed all of the elementary students.

The project that these children were so proud of involved short stories they had written in English, each of which had colorful pictures to go with them. Each of these ten- and eleven-year-olds had been studying English for several years. The tales they had created were surprisingly detailed, so much so that anyone might have assumed that they were written by students living in the United States. I praised their efforts and was rewarded with smiles as well as one of the stories to take home. The teacher explained to me that the next assignment was to become pen pals with children in another country in order to advance their language skills and help them learn more about another culture.

My two-week stay in Costa Rica eventually drew to a close, but I absorbed as much of the native language, culture, and cuisine as possible. I did make it to a rain-forest preserve as well as an amazing cathedral, but the sights that I still hold most dear are of the children at that school who welcomed me into their world with open arms. They couldn't wait to interact with me—even though I was a stranger. They wanted to learn as many details about my life and culture as they could. And, just like me, they were eager to communicate—in Spanish or English—and connect with a fellow human being.

In a sense, this trip to Costa Rica gave me my first glimpse of what a global world we really do live in. I was thousands of miles from home, yet over thirty thousand fellow citizens resided close by. The cities I visited were filled with people from many different countries—living, learning, and working together. And the educators at every level were eagerly striving to prepare their students to interact with the richly diverse world that surrounded them.

UNDERSTANDING THAT DIVERSITY BEGINS WITH ME

As an educator, you don't need to travel to other countries to experience diversity, because as is evident in many cities across America, today's schools and classrooms are true microcosms of the global society in which we live. This should not be a surprise since the United States has been a multicultural, multilingual nation since its inception (Garcia, 2002; Nieto, 2000; Takaki, 1993). In particular, with the well-documented changing demographics of American society during the last half of the twentieth century, multicultural student bodies now populate campuses across this country. Indeed, it is safe to say that culturally and linguistically diverse students will soon be the norm rather than the exception in schools (Banks, 2001; Garcia, 2002; Nieto, 2000).

Looking around your own campus, what kinds of diversity do you experience each and every day? In addition to your students, study the parents, faculty, support staff, and community volunteers. What aspects of culture do you have in common? Since culture includes not only background, ethnicity, language, and experiences but also values, beliefs, rites, and rituals, what similarities and differences can you identify as you interact with these key players in the educational process (Deal & Kennedy, 1982)?

Understanding who you are as an individual is central to the process of becoming a culturally competent educator. You are as unique as each of your students. This may seem like a simplistic statement that should be understood by everyone who works with young people, but this vital concept often gets lost in the overwhelming onslaught of increasing instructional demands, tighter schedules, higher standards and accountability, fiscal constraints, and a myriad of other concerns that today's educators face.

The reality of American education in the twenty-first century involves teaching a diverse student population in increasingly multicultural settings so that they will be prepared to live and work in an intricately connected global economy. Educators are an integral component of the process that allows this type of dynamic learning to take place. "Teachers have a significant role to play in guiding children at all levels to recognize and respect diversity as they interact with other people in and out of school" (Tiedt & Tiedt, 1999, p. 1).

What steps can you take to begin the process of understanding diversity at a deeper level so that you can positively influence the next generation of young people? Below are a few concepts to start you thinking:

- Take a look at your own attitudes and beliefs. Are there any areas where you can identify personal prejudices or situations where you tend to stereotype people?

- What do you know about other culture groups on your campus? Have you read anything about them? Have you attended community events to increase your knowledge and acceptance of these groups?
- Are there hidden institutional practices that you have adopted as your own? For example, does your school site tend to track certain students? Do teachers talk about various culture groups with negative attitudes or low expectations? Does every child have equal access to programs, including sports, clubs, and extracurricular activities?
- Do you attempt to use multiple teaching strategies for diverse learners? For instance, do you implement "scaffolding" techniques in order to link the curriculum to the students' prior knowledge, experience, and understanding?
- How does the curriculum reflect the contributions and perspectives of your school's cultural groups? Do you make an effort to find extra materials, such as poetry, music, recipes, short stories, and posters that reflect your students' backgrounds and give them a historical voice within the academic society?

While you cannot expect to become a cultural expert overnight, you will be surprised at how quickly your efforts toward appreciating diversity will be received by everyone around you—most of all by your students. People like to be understood and accepted for who they are as individuals; this truly is the first step toward building a solid, long-lasting relationship. Once these connections are formed, not only will you be able to teach your academically challenging curriculum, but you will also have the opportunity to share with your students how they too can become better prepared to live in the global world that is their future.

CLASSROOMS AS MINIATURE GLOBAL VILLAGES

There is no doubt that today's schools reflect the increasing diversity evident in American society. A wave of immigration has been transforming many areas of the United States, so much so that "the foreign-born constitute the fastest-growing segment of our population, reaching 24.5 million in 1996, roughly 10 percent of the population" (Garcia,

2002, p. 12). In part this "new immigration" is due to borderless economies, improved communication and technology, and advancements in transportation (Nieto, 2000; Garcia, 2002; Takaki, 1993).

Of course there is no better place to observe the impact of these changing demographics than in American educational institutions. In fact, first- and second-generation immigrant children have been determined to be the fastest-growing segment of the U.S. population under age fifteen (Fix and Passel, 1994). Key areas of the country that are impacted by this increase are California, Texas, New York, Florida, and Illinois, where 82 percent of the immigrant students attend K–12 schools (Garcia, 2002). In addition, demographers project that students of color will make up about 46 percent of the nation's school-age youths by the year 2020 (Banks, 2001).

By the very nature of what is transpiring in society and in schools, many educational settings are already mini–global villages. Rich culture and languages intertwine within the academic curriculum. *This influx of new ways of doing things, thinking about things, and celebrating things enriches our own culture, replenishing and revitalizing it so that it does not become static.* This is what has always been—and will always be—great about the American culture!

Some school sites that I have visited recently have been architecturally designed with this concept in mind. A large, suburban middle school in southern California was built with defined "villages" for the sixth-, seventh-, and eighth-grade students who would make up this campus's student body. The teachers and staff rallied around the idea of the "global village" where each department has its own unique characteristics, yet are all interdependent—choosing to work together for the common good. Even the central quad area was designed for large group gatherings, from meetings to musical concerts.

Even if you are not on a campus that has this kind of people-friendly design, it is still possible to implement the concept of a mini–global village within your own classroom. Below are some ideas to consider:

- Begin the school year or semester by asking the students to research their cultural heritage. They can then write an essay on their findings, draw a picture that symbolizes their family's culture, or bring in something to share about their family background.

- Set aside one bulletin board or wall to be decorated with pictures, posters, maps, key facts, and important heroes from various countries that your students research. Younger children can help design and create these monthly celebrations of nations.
- Organize your room into "minivillages." Rather than table numbers, students can select different countries and design their own table sign. These can be changed periodically throughout the year so the students can learn about other nations, cultures, and languages.
- Play CDs from different countries. Many music stores have international sections where you can choose from a variety of selections.
- Ask a coworker if he or she might be interested in teaming for an international education project. Perhaps you can have the students study a global issue such as deforestation, endangered species, or pollution, and then host a debate on the topic.
- Check with your principal about what type of schoolwide projects have been done to increase global awareness or build a more connected school community. If there haven't been any, suggest one and see whether or not he or she will rally behind your efforts. Maybe you could try a school Olympics program where each class represents a country and then competes in a series of athletic events.

However you decide to start incorporating important issues such as culture, languages, customs, and heritage into your curriculum, you will no doubt find that your ideas will be enthusiastically welcomed, in particular by the diverse students that make up your classroom. If your school site doesn't have a diverse student population, then you can still encourage these kinds of cultural experiences. By doing so, you'll be preparing all of your students for the real world that they live in and will work in one day very soon.

PLUGGING YOUR STUDENTS INTO THE REAL WORLD

When classroom teachers evaluate their own understanding of culture and diversity, they almost innately transfer this self-reflection process on to their students. Educators who comprehend the importance of knowing who they are as individuals and how cultural experiences, language, and heritage impact their daily interactions often are among the first to make their curricula, classrooms, and even school sites more in-clusive. In a sense, they have found the final puzzle pieces that will complete the bigger educational picture.

One of these pieces involves engaging young people in real-world experiences. In order to live and work in the twenty-first century, stu-dents need more of a global view—and they must be prepared to sur-vive in a global economy (Spring, 2002). Educators can help open the eyes of their students to the issues and concerns of other people. Of course, this begins with teaching good communication skills and en-couraging compassion toward their fellow students, other families, and the members of the community. As you work with children to improve their RQ, they will then be able to look at the needs of others on a more global level.

Another essential factor in this new way of teaching young people is cultural competence, that is "the knowledge, attitudes, and skills needed to function in diverse cultural settings" (Banks, 2001, p. 53). Fortunately, many of our nation's schools are diverse by the very na-ture of their demographics, family backgrounds, and cultural commu-nities. In addition, teachers, administrators, and staff members across the country are attempting to create more multicultural school settings. This includes working with staff to have more positive attitudes toward diversity, enhancing materials and curriculum to represent more cul-tural groups, and ensuring that the school culture reflects the diversity of its supporting community (Cole, 1995).

If your school is not making these kinds of strides, then you cer-tainly can implement some of these cultural strategies within your own classroom in order to plug your students into the real world. Here are a few examples of how you might want to begin this process (Tiedt & Tiedt, 1999):

- Try to integrate cultural activities and conversations into your cur-riculum whenever possible.
- Ask your students to share their own cultural experiences.
- Provide opportunities for young people to identify racial, ethnic, and religious groups from around the world.
- Work together to identify examples of stereotyping and prejudice on news programs, within magazine articles, or in literature.

MULTICULTURAL MATTERS

With increased technology and global connections come opportunities to enhance your students' experiences both inside and outside the classroom. Why not implement an international writing program as some students in Ohio and India did (Cushner, 1999)? Several ideas for beginning this type of project are given below, but you can add your own nuances, too. Perhaps the teacher you partner with will have suggestions that will add cultural impact for the kids.

International Cooperative Story-Writing Activity

1. Search the Internet for possible contacts for your class. Send e-mails to several teachers to determine whether or not they are interested in having their students correspond with yours via the Internet and even international mail.
2. Have your students start to write a creative story, but stop them at the halfway point. Then send these off to the students that they will partner with and allow them to finish the stories. Be sure to set aside enough class time to share the completed tales.
3. Next, have the partner group begin a new story. Ask their teacher to send them unfinished for your students to complete this time around.

Extension for Elementary Students: Send drawings along with the story.
Extension for Secondary Students: Send recordings of your voices, photographs, and personal biographies to build deeper relationships.

- Have a debate on the impact of racism and discrimination on specific groups such as senior citizens, the disabled, or refugees.

Without negating the importance of classroom experiences, educators must also begin to expand students' horizons by letting them experience more about the world than they will through the basic curriculum. For example, you can bring individuals into your classroom who can share stories of their own lives and experiences. These people may include parents, staff, volunteers, and community members. If your school has a volunteer program, you may be able to enlist the help of others fairly easily; if not, then you can start a volunteer list of your own—perhaps even on back-to-school night.

You may also want to involve your students in the surrounding community. For younger students, field trips are beneficial because you can include parents and guardians in these events. Find out if there is a local business that you could visit as a class and that fits into a lesson that you are planning. Several years ago a science teacher told me about a field trip she planned to a local toy store. It had a special section dedicated to telescopes, partly because the owner enjoyed astronomy. So one afternoon, the class walked to the store and then had the chance to hear about the mechanics of the telescope. To the kids' delight, as a gift from the owner, they each received a map of constellations that glowed in the dark.

Older students can become involved in community service activities in and around their neighborhood. A high school English teacher found out about a local park that needed trees to be planted in a barren area. Since her students had been reading short stories related to environmental issues, she felt that this would be an excellent activity to conclude the unit. Best of all, this group of teenagers enthusiastically agreed. They even gave up a Saturday morning to meet at the park to plant the saplings!

There are some teachers who aren't sure where to find ideas such as these to incorporate into their curriculum, but once you start to think more globally, ideas for these types of activities will seem to surface out of nowhere. For instance, as you drive to work, you may pay more attention to what is happening in the neighborhood, what new businesses are opening, or which areas look as though they need some extra "TLC." Your students can also be the source of inspiration; many times they will talk about community events or clubs that they are involved in.

Finally, don't forget about technology as one of your resources for plugging students into the bigger world around them. Some of the best cultural experiences that you can give students include interacting with other young people from around the globe. Fortunately, this kind of experience is far easier to come by today than ever before thanks to computers, which provide methods that are much less expensive than using traditional mail services. As you and your students attempt to get plugged into real-world experiences, all of you will be making great strides toward becoming more culturally competent.

LEARNING TO LOOK THROUGH "DIFFERENT LENSES"

Joel Vasquez beamed with pleasure as he relayed details about an experience he had in the first-grade classroom he shared with sixteen six-year-olds. As an educator who believed in teaching children about acceptance and inclusion from an early age, Mr. Vasquez strove to teach his students how positive attitudes and treatment of others really makes the world a better place. And on this particular Wednesday, it seemed that at least part of these lessons had finally sunk in.

"Anika came up to me this morning and said that she'd like to see Justin have a successful day at school. She told me that she wanted to help him do this!"

Joel promptly explained how his students were arranged in cooperative groups of four and that Anika and Justin had been seated at the separate tables. He also informed me that because of Justin's ADHD, he had been in and out of these groups for months due to behavior problems. Currently Justin had a separate table near the front of the class.

"At any rate, I decided to take Anika up on her offer. I moved another student to a different table and let Justin join Table Three. I kept an eye on him, but Anika had things well in hand. She gently tapped him on the shoulder when he started to talk or fiddle with his pencil box. She and her tablemates also checked to make sure that he was on the correct page during reading time. To be honest with you, I didn't think that Justin would ever be able to make it through an entire day without getting his name on the board—but he did it!"

When I asked Mr. Vasquez why he thought this day was different than all of the others, his response was insightful.

"Oh, I definitely think that our discussions on inclusion have had an impact, and so have the ones that we've had as a class about how important it is to take care of our neighbors—to reach out and help. But to be perfectly frank, this success is all about one child being willing to step up and try something that she's never done before. Anika made a difference in Justin's life today; no telling what she'll be able to do tomorrow!"

What Mr. Vasquez had witnessed was the power that young people have when they look beyond themselves into the bigger world around them. Although the world for a six-year-old like Anika may seem relatively small, she saw the need of a fellow student and rose to the occasion. She looked past his behavior problems—and even how the other students had been reacting to him—and her action plan paid off! She envisioned what was possible because she had been taught by her tenacious teacher how to look at life a little bit differently.

As you work with your students to develop the skills necessary to relate to people—all people—in the community in which they live, you must begin by addressing how they currently relate to people, places, and events. Talking to your students, of whatever age level, will help you assess their relationship skills as well as their attitudes about others. By providing opportunities within the classroom for students to interact, you'll quickly discover what strengths and weakness they have when it comes to relating with others. Today's schools must also involve "students in curricula that enhance human relationships, critical thinking, and civic responsibility, . . . examining how individuals think through their ideas and actions and make decisions " (Garcia, 2002, p. 70).

Once you have identified the positive ways that your students relate to one another, you can build on these strengths throughout your own curriculum. For instance, if you have a group that is accepting of different ideas and opinions, try to incorporate more discussion time into your lesson plan. If many of your students have had cross-cultural experiences, find opportunities to let them share these experiences whenever possible.

Likewise, your students' weaknesses in the area of tolerance toward diversity must be addressed. Perhaps you can infuse your course content with information, stories, and experiences that offer "new perspectives, frames of reference, and values" (Banks, 2001, p. 234). If your textbooks and materials do not offer a wide range of stories about or examples of various ethnic groups, particularly those represented by your student population, then hunt for some stories that you can include on a regular basis. Your school librarian or a resource specialist in your district can aid in this search.

The ultimate goal is for you to allow your students to look at themselves, one another, and the world around them from a wide variety of perspectives. By doing so, you will let them develop the skills necessary to interact with any individual they will encounter throughout their journey in life. As Banks (2001) stresses, when you give young people a chance to become culturally competent, you are also helping them to "view events, situations, and problems from the perspectives of different ethnic and nationality groups" (p. 53).

Learning to look through different lenses is all about seeing the world from varying points of view. In other words, life is not all about "me"; it is also about the wonderfully unique and diverse people who make up classrooms, campuses, counties, countries, and the global community! As you catch a glimpse of this bigger picture of education, then you will be more than ready to assist your students in opening their own eyes a little wider. This process, as Takaki (1993) eloquently summarizes, takes time, effort, tenacity, and even a bit of bravery: "America's dilemma has been our resistance to ourselves—our denial of our immensely varied selves. But we have nothing to fear but our fear of our own diversity" (p. 427).

OFFERING HOPE IN A SOMETIMES HEARTLESS WORLD

During the weeks that I was working on this chapter, I took a break one evening to watch television with my family. We ended up finding a sports program (with two sons and a husband, this is not an unusual occurrence for me) about the life of Donovan McNabb. If, like me, you are somewhat clueless when it comes to professional athletes, Mr. McNabb is a fantastic quarterback in the NFL. His stats are amazing—and so was his struggle to become a quarterback in the first place.

As this hour-long sports history began to unfold, the narrator showed clips of a young Donovan and his family—who were black—trying to fit in in a predominately white suburban neighborhood of Chicago. Before they even moved into the newly purchased home, vandals attacked in an attempt to scare them away. During Donovan's teenage years, some coaches couldn't envision him playing quarterback because he was African American. Why? Their answer was simple—and shameful—there just weren't many African Americans in that position. Sadly this same stereotyping—and racism—followed Mr. McNabb all the way through college and into his professional career.

I sat transfixed for the entire hour, partly because I was in a state of shock and disbelief. It was March 2004, and I was watching a discussion on whether or not professional football was ready for African

American quarterbacks! Questions whirled in my mind—Is this for real? Can we still be talking about this kind of topic fifty years after desegregation? Didn't the Civil Rights movement happen over forty—not four—years ago?

Yet this scenario is tragically real, and this is part of the sometimes heartless world that many students face in the twenty-first century. There are people who have a problem with ethnicity. There are others who don't like any language other than their own being spoken—and there are still invisible barriers that exist where we think that they have already been broken down.

This problem, however, extends to much deeper regions of the human experience. *At the very core of the issue is the acceptance or rejection of whatever an individual deems as "other."* Earlier in the story about Justin, his "otherness" was that he struggled with ADHD. His behavior problems had led to his separation—physically and emotionally—from his classmates. In that same group of first graders, a young girl named Hillary wears a hearing device. Her "otherness" is obvious and could have caused her to be ostracized by her fellow students.

In *Resounding Voices: School Experiences of People from Diverse Ethnic Backgrounds* (Boutte, 2002), Carol Marxen tells her own story about growing up in rural America. As a young girl, she experienced what it was like to be known as one of "those people who live on a dairy farm" (p. 133). Her classmates saw her as an oddity and referred to where she lived as the "boondocks." Yet her parents worried about her socializing with the city kids, "those people who live in Park Center" (p. 134). For Ms. Marxen, like many students who live in small towns across this country, their "otherness" is simply where and how they live.

Carol Marxen, however, used her experiences of feeling different— as part of a category that some people might not typically define as "other"—into something powerful. While becoming an educator, her eyes were opened to the need to teach children how to interact and accept each other—differences and all. "Only when individuals explore their diverse roots and branches can they fully understand the whole, and only when individuals respect differences can we become one society" (Boutte, 2002).

In the cases of Justin, Hillary, and Carol, what could have been dividing differences—even in first grade—became diverse opportunities for increased compassion, understanding, and unity. Justin and Hillary's teacher made a concerted effort to instill these concepts in the primary grades so that they, like seeds planted in springtime, would blossom in the seasons still to come. By actively engaging his students' relationship quotients, Mr. Vasquez guided these youngsters as they interacted with one another and learned to accept one another's' differences.

For educators, it is not only our duty but it should also be our moral resolve to offer hope to all children about their present as well as their future lives. *It is possible to teach children the skills necessary to interact with others in a positive, productive manner!* Teachers can do this by actively addressing issues of diversity (Howard, 1999). Schools can encourage these ideals by providing curriculum and activities that help prepare students for real-world experiences (Comer, Ben-Avie, Haynes, & Joyner, 1999).

Yes, it really is the twenty-first century! The global future is right here, right now. Educators who are working in today's school communities know that there is no more time to talk about diversity, and those of us who work with young people can no longer afford to wait patiently for someone to develop a compassionate curriculum. The cost of emotional illiteracy is too high—increased aggression, social problems, withdrawal, depression, drug abuse, violence, and crime are just a few of the ways today's youth are crying out for help (Goleman, 1995).

Teaching young people how to connect well with others and how to interact daily in positive, meaningful ways should be at the core of whatever you do in the classroom. By providing students with multiple opportunities to look at lives outside of their own, to understand concepts such as empathy and acceptance, and to break down the invisible walls of stereotyping and intolerance, you will truly be offering hope (Goleman, 1995). And it is also through this process that students and educators alike will appreciate their own diversity as well as their common humanity (Boutte, 2002; Howard, 1999).

CLASSROOM CONUNDRUM

About five minutes into a new group project, one of your students comes up to you with a disgruntled look on his face. When you ask

Kevin how you can help him, he quietly whispers that he doesn't want to work with "those kids" at his table. Glancing toward the back of the room, you realize that "those kids" he's referring to are the small group of ELL students who have been integrated into your class. Although you know that Kevin could certainly benefit from this opportunity to work with these classmates, you also realize he has a history of behavior problems. Is it worth the effort to keep Kevin where he is, or should you simply replace him with a student who has more empathy for your ELL kids? Shouldn't you be thinking of these language learners, too? Won't they have an easier time without Kevin in the mix?

Refer to appendix A, "Potential Solutions for Classroom Conundrums," at the end of the book for ideas on how to answer these questions.

CHAPTER 9

Staying Connected to Yourself, Your Family, and Your Career

Jerry Black gripped the handle of his briefcase tightly as he headed toward the high school that had been so welcoming when he first interviewed there ten years earlier. Today, like so many days recently, he looked grimly at the large, gray edifice, hardly noticing the noisy adolescents who swarmed around him as they unloaded from the school buses. His heart felt heavy as he trudged to his mailbox and then on to his classroom. He tried to remember those early days when he seemed to have more of a spring in his step, eagerly awaiting the start of another morning with his students.

Several of his colleagues watched Jerry's solemn progress through the office and out into the courtyard. Sipping their coffee, three of them contrived possible theories for Mr. Black's obvious change over the past year.

"He's simply burned out. Ten years of teaching can do that to you," the woodshop teacher stated knowingly. The art teacher nodded in agreement.

"It's these ridiculous contract negotiations," replied a fellow math teacher. "They have us all stressed. Did you know we might have to strike if things don't get resolved soon?"

As Jerry Black slowly opened his classroom door and turned on the lights, he had no idea that one of the school counselors was also talking about him. She'd slipped into the principal's office to discuss a few matters before the school day started, and one of them was the increasing number of calls she had been receiving from unhappy parents.

"What seems to be the problem with Jerry?" Mr. Jefferson queried.

"I'm not sure, but four parents have called in the past few days to complain about his apathy. The students feel that he doesn't care about how they are doing—or at least that's what they're telling their parents."

"Well, I guess I will have to talk to him," the principal replied with some hesitation. "Maybe I should have reassigned him to the computer lab like he requested last spring. The problem is that he has little background in computers, and the younger teacher candidates coming out of the universities are more prepared to teach technology. Can you imagine how many workshops we'd have to send him to in order to get him up to speed?"

Ms. Simmons looked down at the pile of messages that lay in her lap. Silently she wished that they had at least given Jerry Black the chance to teach the new computer program. Something was definitely wrong with him, but she didn't know what. Why, he'd been the campus's outstanding teacher just three years earlier! What could have happened to such an outstanding educator?

Meanwhile Jerry Black stared at the clock as the minute hand quickly approached the half hour. He took another drink of his coffee in a vain attempt to reinvigorate himself before he had to let the students in the door, but his mind raced with thoughts of his teenage son's newly discovered drinking problem, his wife's job loss two months earlier, and the mounting bills that needed to be paid by the end of the month. The reality of these crises far overshadowed what his colleagues concluded must be the causes of his sudden burnout.

IT'S NOT BUSINESS . . . IT'S PERSONAL

Unfortunately, Jerry Black's situation is not unique. Educators encounter the stresses of life like everyone else in society. As this new century begins to unfold, stress levels seem to be at an all-time high (Burmark & Fournier, 2003). The pace of living in an increasingly global world only compounds the normal pressures of day-to-day living. In addition, twenty-four-hour satellite media provide people with an overwhelming and unhealthy awareness of natural disasters, political unrest, and international terrorist threats (Weil, 1997).

The encouraging news is that much of what enhances balanced, happy living is within reach for most people. This simple philosophy centers around one key concept: personal responsibility. *While you may not (and actually should not) be able to control the actions of others, you can work on your own thoughts, feelings, perceptions, and reactions to life events.* Even though circumstances around you may seem out of control, you can cultivate positive responses to them.

For those in the field of education, however, this type of personal balance is becoming more of a daunting task. The mantras of "school improvement" and "educational reform" don't mention the increased workloads or the anxiety levels for everyone behind the scenes attempting to meet new standards and raise test scores (Sornson & Scott, 1997; Burmark & Fournier, 2003). There is a cost beyond what can be reported in federal, state, and local budgets, but sadly, the price involves personal fatigue, burnout, health problems, and even death (Burmark & Fournier, 2003).

Years ago I joined a school district that had an outstanding reputation; indeed, it was reported to be the best in the entire county. I quickly learned the reason for the rising test scores and nationally recognized schools: the teachers, staff members, and administration all worked—or perhaps I should say ran—at an extremely accelerated rate. Their daily existence was like stepping on a treadmill going full speed, and everyone who became part of the team was expected to jump on and keep up!

The trouble is that no one—even the best and brightest educators—can maintain this type of grueling schedule for very long. In fact, about three years into this teaching experience, a large insurance company refused to cover the district employees any longer. Why? There were simply too many stress-related illnesses! The district not only had more of its workforce visiting doctors for a variety of health issues than did other districts, but it also had one of the largest chunks of prescription medicine claims. These factors are not unique to teaching, but they contribute to the nationwide statistics that show 70 to 90 percent of doctor visits in the United States are stress related (Burmark & Fournier, 2003).

Perhaps part of the problem is the modern belief that the work we do defines who we are, when in reality this concept should be reversed. *Who we are should define what we do.* A person's unique talents and abilities add character and quality to a specific position. It is your own creative flair and charisma that enhance your curriculum and classroom environment—not the other way around!

Another school district I encountered adopted a motto that sums up the sad state of some educational institutions today. Proudly displayed in their central office was a banner that read "Education Is Our Business." Upon further investigation, it became evident that this district was run more like a savvy corporation than a compassionate environment that cared for children. It had plenty of financial reserves and strictly followed federal and state mandates. The administrators intensely examined the schools to ensure that each of them followed the rigorous standards that had been established. It wasn't that the attempts at accountability were inappropriate, but somewhere in the thrust toward this corporate mentality, the professionals in charge had forgotten what should be paramount: *education is all about the people involved in the process.* Not only were the staff members burning out at every level, but even worse, so were the students!

Whatever the philosophy of your state, district, or school, as an educator you have the choice of how you intend to walk through your personal and professional life. Will teaching be more about the students than the latest standards? Can the people in your life take precedence over timelines and deadlines? And, most importantly, are you willing to take proper care of yourself so that you will not only enjoy your career, but also be able to experience real joy and satisfaction throughout your entire journey in life?

TAKING TIME FOR YOUR RELATIONSHIPS

Accepting personal responsibility for how your life is going to operate must entail a personal worldview. In other words, as you start to look more at *who* you are, *who* you want to become, *who* the essential people in your life are, and *who* you want to focus on in your profession, it will become crystal clear that all of these core issues deal with relationships. This brings you back full circle to the main theme presented in chapter 1: *Relationships Are the Center of the Universe!*

Taking time to nourish as well as relish the relationships that are already in place in your life is critical to your own personal contentment and feelings of well-being (Jenson, 1998; Burmark & Fournier, 2003). Unfortunately, these are the exact same connections people begin to cut back on and actually shun when their lives become busy, stressful, or overwhelming. Yet friends and family members should be part of your daily support system, and they ought to be your first line of defense when the going gets tough.

Who are some of the key players in your personal life? Take a few moments to check this relationship inventory. You might even want to star the ones that are truly integral to your feelings of well-being:

- ☐ Parent(s)
- ☐ Brother(s)
- ☐ Sister(s)
- ☐ Best friend
- ☐ Spouse
- ☐ Children
- ☐ Roommate
- ☐ Minister or Rabbi
- ☐ Mentor
- ☐ Next-door neighbor(s)
- ☐ Exercise partner
- ☐ College buddy
- ☐ Godparent
- ☐ Aunt, uncle, or other relative
- ☐ Coworker
- ☐ Counselor

Who else should be added to your list? Why? What is it that makes them integral to your very existence? (And, by the way, have you let them know lately how special they are to you?) Can you call one or more of them on a good day to share your exhilaration and excitement about life? Are they equally willing to listen and give helpful advice when everything seems to be falling apart?

The people who you have identified really are your personal "circle of friends." They can add color, beauty, and a sweet aroma to your life, much like a bouquet of fresh flowers brought in from the garden. The funny thing about flowers, though, is that they don't grow well on their own—they need your regular attention. And they won't pound on your door and demand an entrance! You have to make an effort to connect with them in order for them to become part of your world.

Building better relationships is part of the balance that all educators must develop in their lives—especially if they truly hope to enjoy a long, satisfying career. "Those of us who teach need to consciously nourish our own joy and energy for what we do. . . . [W]e must proactively guard against letting the job . . . diminish our zest for teaching and our enthusiasm for the individuals we teach" (Sornson & Scott, 1997, p. 21).

Healthy, loving people can help overcome many of the negative aspects of living in an imperfect world. Yes, there will be times when someone you were close to may hurt you, but that doesn't mean that you should avoid contact with other friends or family members. Actually, by identifying those who you really do trust and can rely on, you will be able to focus more of your time and attention on developing these positive relationships.

Eastern philosophy has taught people for centuries that all of life should be lived in balance. A few years ago I observed this ideal being visually displayed by an acrobatic act at a Cirque du Soleil performance. Seven nimble men carefully formed a human pyramid of interlocking limbs. As each member climbed, contorted his body, and found his balancing point, the audience gasped in amazement. Surely, they would topple over at any moment . . . yet due to their graceful teamwork, they were able to defy gravity itself.

This is the fundamental reason for relationships! As you work together with the significant others in your life, you will be more grounded and stable than you can ever imagine. When you try to reach new heights, someone will be there to offer you a helping hand. If life gets difficult, you will find a friend ready to steady and support you. Perhaps the most pleasant surprise of all will be the discovery that those around you really depend upon the balance that you offer in their lives as well.

TAKING TIME FOR YOU

Time is one of the most precious yet elusive parts of life. Everyone has the same twenty-four hours to spend, but at the end of the day, some people cannot fathom how all of those minutes slipped away from them. Even as I began my morning, intending to start writing this section by 8:00 A.M., there were distractions. A lunch needed to be made, then one son needed a ride to school. On this journey, I discovered the gas gauge was almost on empty. Once I returned to my office, there were three messages waiting—and, oops, I hadn't checked my e-mail yet. A few of those messages needed prompt responses. Finally I turned on the computer, glancing at the clock: 11:25 A.M.!

And this is just one of many mornings that start this way. You can probably relate. After teaching a full day and giving all that you can to your students, you still have other demands that must be met. Groceries need to be purchased. Errands must be run. Traffic congestion only adds to your stress as you try to make a meeting at your child's school or attend an evening function. Laundry? Maybe you'll get to it after you gobble down some dinner and wade through the stack of paperwork you had to bring home.

As you know, you aren't alone in this daily balancing act. Everyone's lives have become increasingly busy and fast-paced, no thanks to all of the technology that was supposed to save us time. So when agendas get packed, work becomes overwhelming, and people put demands on you, what is usually the first thing that you give up? If you are like other educators, it usually will be any plans that you may have made to take care of yourself. Unfortunately, this type of budget cut won't help you in the long run. As Dr. Andrew Weil (1997) explains, your health and well-being will eventually be shortchanged too.

Part of the educator's modern-day dilemma about self-care is the lack of discussion about its importance within the profession. After perusing many educational journals and textbooks in my library, I found only one that really broached the subject at all. Not surprisingly, this is also true of many of the popular leadership development books. *Leadership and the One-Minute Manager: Increasing Effectiveness through Situational Leadership* (Blanchard, Zigarmi, & Zigarmi, 1985) talks about how to best manage your day, but mentions nothing about setting aside time to rejuvenate. *Good to Great: Why Some Companies Make the Leap and Others Don't* (Collins, 2001) offers excellent advice on how to enhance the nuts and bolts of business, but gives no information on such vital parts of success as rest and relaxation.

Speaking of this concept, what have you done for yourself lately? Or, as Burmark and Fournier (2003) put it, what things have you done to refill your personal ATM? "We all have emotional and psychological

MULTICULTURAL MATTERS

One of the best ways to reflect on personal growth is to keep a journal of life experiences. Although you may have used this tool in the past, busy educators often get distracted and forget how vital the process can truly be. Purchase a notebook or journal that you can keep on your desk or nightstand. At the end of each day, jot down thoughts about how things are going both personally and professionally. Here are a few questions to get you started:

- What is the best thing that happened today?
- Am I connecting with my students as I had hoped? What relationships are going well? Which ones should I focus on this week?
- What new thing did I learn about myself this week?
- When I had that new multicultural encounter, how did I feel? Was there any personal prejudice that I should be aware of? How can I improve on this?
- When I read that professional journal, what article spoke to me most? Why? How can I explore this area more if it is so interesting to me?
- How are my interpersonal relationships going? Which person means the most to me right now? Why?
- What fun, frivolous, or spontaneous activity have I done lately just for me? Why did I enjoy it so much?

---

personal 'bank accounts' from which we make frequent withdrawals every day. These need deposits as well, and, happily they're easy and very rewarding to make" (Burmark & Fournier, 2003, p. 10).

Review the checklist below. See how many items represent what you have done to help refill your personal reservoir recently:

- took an afternoon walk or jog
- read a book just for fun
- slept in late one weekend
- took a class in a personal area of interest
- met a friend for a leisurely dinner
- picked up a new CD to listen to
- slipped away to a matinee to view a new movie

- scheduled a weekend getaway for a change of scenery
- went to a ballgame with a buddy

Were you able to find at least one activity that you did just for yourself? Is there anything else that you could add? If not, then take a few minutes right now to think about something that would really be refreshing and relaxing. To be an excellent educator—not to mention a well-balanced individual—you must get a new perspective on self-care. As an old friend reminded me years ago when my father was ill, my children were young, and my workload was demanding, "if you don't take care of yourself, who else is going to do it?"

By taking small increments of time to be quiet, listen to your own thoughts, reflect on life, take in the beauty of the world, and enjoy the little blessings that each day brings, you will naturally become a better person—not to mention a better professional. You will also be healthier—and happier! "Health is wholeness and balance, an inner reliance that allows you to meet the demands of living without being overwhelmed. . . . [O]ptimal health should also bring with it a sense of strength and joy" (Weil, 1997, p. 13).

LEARNING FOR A LIFETIME

I love the story told by Mimi Brodsky Chenfeld about a fellow professional, Sister Miriam, she met years ago at an education conference. They often caught up with one another at these types of events. One year Ms. Chenfeld leaned over and whispered, "Sister Miriam, this is my thirtieth year of teaching!" Without missing a beat, her friend replied, "This is my sixtieth! The first thirty years are the hardest!" (Sornson & Scott, 1997, p. 4).

Can you imagine having that type of attitude after sixty years of working with children? What kinds of lessons had Sister Miriam learned along the way that kept her so enthusiastic about education? How had she been inspired to keep going and giving year in and year out? What allowed her to maintain balance in a demanding profession that had changed so dramatically over six decades?

Educators today can certainly take something valuable away from Sister Miriam's example. Teaching is more than a job—it is a calling, and callings don't stop when a bell rings or the clock strikes a particular hour. In fact, educating young people truly is a life-long effort, because it takes time to hone the skills of this craft and pass on all of that learning to the next generation.

Do educators ever really reach a point when they feel that they have done it perfectly? No, they would probably relate to the world-renowned artist Michelangelo, whose motto was "I am still learning" (Sornson & Scott, 1997). Most teachers tend to agree with the master painter: there is and always will be room for improvement. Exceptional educators usually say things such as, "That activity that I did this morning could be improved if I just tweaked it this way" or "I can't wait to attend that conference so I can get more fabulous ideas to enrich my program at school!"

This may be a large part of why you selected the teaching profession in the first place. You like learning, and you plan on learning for a lifetime. Educational experts concur that this is how it should be: "The professional educator is constantly on an endless journey of looking for new and better ideas, new information, and improved skills to succeed with students" (Wong & Wong, 1998, p. 296); "teachers (individually and collectively) must develop the habits and skills of continuous inquiry and learning, always seeking new ideas inside and outside their own settings" (Fullan, 1994, p. 81).

From the business perspective of education, this type of learning is described as "professional development." In addition to encouraging teachers, administrators, and support staff to continue to explore and expand their knowledge base, every state across America has defined standards in terms of what must be done to maintain credentials and certifications. Although research often drives the specific types of training, in-services, and workshops offered to educators year to year, national trends and local needs should also determine what issues, curriculum changes, and instructional methods should be addressed (Odden, 1995).

The inevitable changes brought about by the increasing knowledge base and expanding technology, not to mention transformations in society, should be enough encouragement for you to want to keep up with your dynamic profession. "Just as change is an undeniable part of life, it also is an undeniable part of teaching and learning. Consequently, it makes sense for educators to learn how change occurs, how to facilitate it, and how individuals respond to it"(Jensen & Kiley, 2000, p. 496).

There is an equally essential component to lifelong learning that is seldom addressed in professional and educational research. This involves understanding more about the personal side of life in addition to the professional! *Improving your content and curriculum are important endeavors, but they are not as essential as comprehending what makes you and others tick.* The paperwork should never be more important than the personal connections that you will make with your students, fellow staff members, friends, and family!

If you don't believe me, then tell me what you learned when you were in sixth grade. Do you recall even one single lesson plan your teacher worked on and carefully taught that year? If you're like me, you probably haven't a clue. But do you remember your sixth grade teacher—who he or she was, whether or not he or she ever smiled at you, how you felt when you entered his or her classroom? I do, and thank you Mr. Bean for making it a fun-filled and exciting year of learning!

You can try this question on any other adult—or student for that matter. More than likely the individuals will talk more about the teachers than the content—the learning environment more than the actual lesson plan. What does this tell you, the educator? Perhaps you are beginning to see that people—and that includes you—are at the core of the teaching/learning continuum. If this is true, then doesn't it make sense for you to spend more time and energy caring for others than fretting over standards, curriculum changes, and district demands?

I particularly like the conclusion that Burmark and Fournier (2003) arrived at when they were asked why they spend so much of their time focusing on relationships when there are so many other practical needs in education. They summarize their beliefs this way: "the true purpose of education is fundamentally to empower and enrich the human heart. What does it profit a teacher to gain a mind but lose a heart? Clearly, the practical curricula of learning is critically important, but no more so than is fostering a loving and enlightened heart" (p. 88).

And that is how it should be for you. What good does it do to only feed your mind with more knowledge and information when your spirit is depleted and your soul is weary? Taking time to rest, relax, and reflect at different points during the year is essential for educators to practice all throughout their careers (Wilke, 2003). These "self-care breaks" actually result in exponential learning—especially in the area of personal growth that will eventually enhance your professional life as well. Some important things that you might want to spend more time investigating include:

- areas of interest outside of your career
- thoughts and feelings about the people in your life
- ideas on how to improve the quality of your life
- ways to reach out to others in your world
- beliefs and values that have strengthened this year
- things that you would like to read about, study, or experience
- dreams that you have left unrealized
- plans for the future that you want to begin executing

Learning about you is the best place to start this entire journey of developing better relationships both inside and outside of the classroom! As Wong and Wong (1998) suggest, "Get in touch with your own magnificence" (p. 320). Once you begin discovering what drives you, what your passions are, and what revitalizes you, then you'll be ready to nurture and improve the other critical connections in your world. And, as naturally as a well-tended garden, these interpersonal interactions will take off and bloom with vigor and vitality.

Wouldn't it be wonderful to make it through thirty years in this career with an outlook like Sister Miriam's? Can you imagine reaching this point in your educational journey feeling that you are ready for a few more decades? No matter how long you've been in this profession, or how long you hope to keep going, your own attitude about learning and life starts today. What will your motto—or for that matter, your modus operandi—be?

IT REALLY WILL BE A WONDERFUL WORLD

Despite many of the problems and pitfalls of today's global society, as educators we have the opportunity to interact with young people on a daily basis and be revitalized by their fresh insights in addition to their hopes and dreams for the future. You have the chance to positively impact the next generation with ideas and ideals that may truly change the world. Most of all, as a teacher you are able to continue growing and learning throughout your lifetime, discovering more and more about yourself and all the diverse people who make up your community!

Although Jerry Black's situation appeared bleak after only ten years in the classroom, he was surrounded by compassionate individuals who realized they needed to reach out and help their fellow traveler in the educational journey. Tim Nesbitt, the woodshop teacher, stopped by that day after school "just to chat." Jerry tried to send him away with a few simple replies to his queries, but Tim was persistent, persuading his coworker to join him after work at a local coffee shop. That's when Jerry opened up about his current problems.

And Tim didn't try to solve his coworker's dilemmas; instead he listened for an hour—and Jerry felt a little better by sharing with a friend. The next day, Mr. Jefferson came to Jerry's classroom during his prep period and asked if he could take a quick stroll around the block. During their brief walk, the principal told Jerry about a time when he was a teacher struggling with some issues. Without prying into Jerry's affairs, this caring administrator let him know that his office door would always be open if Jerry ever wanted to talk. He also reminded Jerry about the district's wellness office, where he could receive extra assistance in a confidential format.

By the end of that week, Jerry had met with the support person at the wellness office, who gave him some names and phone numbers to get help for his son. He stayed after school one day to share some of what was going on with Mr. Jefferson, and he thanked Ms. Simmons for the nice note she'd left in his mailbox two days earlier. The counselor was relieved to see a small sparkle back in Jerry's blue eyes.

The transformation process took some time, but about two months later a visitor to Mr. Black's classes would never have known there had been such a crisis in this exceptional educators' life. His students once again bounced into his room, eager to talk to their teacher about the previous night's homework, the latest movie they'd seen, and even some of their own personal problems. Jerry Black, with the assistance of key people around him, had his life back under control, and he'd learned the invaluable lesson of how critical it is to take care of himself so he can indeed reach out to others.

When you first started reading this book, perhaps you had some inkling of how essential relationships are to your everyday existence, but hopefully now you've gotten a glimpse of the bigger picture: *connecting with others is critical to happiness, well-being, and ultimately, success in life.* And the RQ must begin with you. The initial stages of this process includes understanding who you are and how you relate to others, then it continues to discovering more ways to interact on a more interpersonal level with the important people in your life. Finally, by putting these simple ideas into practice as you walk through your entire journey in life, you will hone your relationship skills so they become a natural part of who you are as a person and a professional.

Having the mind-set that relationships are the center of your universe really can reshape the world as you know it! Imagine starting each day thinking more about the people that you're going to impact as opposed to the pain in your left shoulder, the problem with your irrigation system, or the price of gasoline. Would caring about the connections that you're forming with your students and colleagues help alleviate any anxiety over the curriculum change that is coming next year or the new standardized test that you must make time for in your already busy schedule?

This RQ view will not be a panacea, but it does offer a new paradigm that will lighten your load and lift your spirit to places that you might not have visited since childhood. This insight hit me like a pleasant breeze on a balmy day while I watched a group of kindergartners during recess. Those five- and six-year-olds could care less about the problems outside their playground; they were too busy jumping, skipping, hopping, and laughing with one another. When the bell rang, they held hands and lined up outside their classroom, eagerly waiting for their teacher to take them back into the magical world of learning.

It wasn't the three Rs that inspired these new learners to reengage with the educational process. Instead, it was all about relationships— their relationships with one another and with their teacher. "The motivation for teaching is inherently a sense of purpose, a kind of mission . . . where the *why* (teaching, encouraging, and empowering every learner) is every bit as important as the *what* (curriculum) and *how* (methodology)" (Burmark & Fournier, 2003, p. 93).

The academic achievement and success of all students must be among the major goals of the educational process, but matters of the mind must be balanced with those of the heart. Children will come to school when they know they are truly cared for; young people will want to perform at their best when they feel a personal connection with their teachers.

The same is true for the professionals and other key players involved in the business of educating young minds and hearts. Teachers, support staff, and administrators will naturally enjoy being at school when they have formed strong connections with their colleagues. Parents want to be involved at school sites that make an effort to build good relationships with them. And everyone, no matter what their ethnic background, religion, or language, will feel welcomed on a campus that embraces the multicultural forces at work in our global society.

Yes, it really is—and will be—a wonderful world when "relationship" becomes part of your personal motto and everyday experience. *The connections that you are forming right now really will make a difference in, around, and beyond your school community!* This piece of the educational—and relational—puzzle is finally yours for the keeping. Go ahead, put it in its proper place—then get ready for the exciting changes that will happen in all your relationships.

CLASSROOM CONUNDRUM

This year you've been assigned to work with a team teacher who is known for her outstanding program and involvement in the district. You're excited to learn from this leader, and the school year starts out well, except that Kathy McKnight likes to work long hours after school and on Saturdays, and she expects you to adopt the same philosophy. Although you don't mind putting in the extra time needed to keep your classroom running smoothly, you discover that Kathy resents the fact that you leave some days before 5 P.M. in order to exercise, attend the class you signed up for last spring, or even meet a friend for dinner. Kathy also insists that you have planning meetings during your lunch period, which means that you don't have the freedom to eat with your colleagues. What can you do with this overzealous coworker? Can you confront Kathy without ruining your relationship? Will you be able to share the fact that you're indeed dedicated to this profession, but you also need to have more balance in your life?

Refer to appendix A, "Potential Solutions for Classroom Conundrums," at the end of the book for ideas on how to answer these questions.

Potential Solutions for Classroom Conundrums

Although there can be multiple answers for these types of puzzling situations, the following suggestions are provided to help you think through the types of dilemmas that arise in real school communities. They are offered to you as possible ideas to assist in your own educational journey.

CHAPTER 1

This educator is not alone in her experiences. Many teachers, both young and old, novice and experienced, can become overwhelmed with the demands of today's school communities. When it comes to relationships, this teacher needs to realize that she must take care of herself first and foremost. She should stay in touch with those closest to her—her family and friends. Whatever changes and challenges she faces, these tried and true relationships will be her best source of support. Next, she might develop a friendship or two with other staff members. By doing so, she will have someone else to bounce professional concerns and ideas off of at the end of the day (as she is doing with you in this conundrum).

Finally, as she begins the school year, her next priority must be her students. Building good connections with them now will pay dividends down the road. Forming these relationships will involve interacting with her students' parents or guardians, but there will be plenty of opportunity to make connections with this part of the community as the year gets going.

CHAPTER 2

As frustrating as this type of scenario may seem, what often draws people into education is the desire to assist each and every child who crosses their paths. This young man may be a challenge, but he is not beyond help! Although you might be out of fresh ideas, there are numerous educators around you who may have some new ones. Talk the situation over with a fellow teacher or administrator. See what things they might have done in similar circumstances and try a few of these in the coming days.

In addition, if you haven't contacted the parents or guardians about your concerns yet, now is the time to do so. You may even discover that there are issues at home that are causing some of the aloofness that you are experiencing at school. If nothing else, you will have apprised the caretakers of the problem so that they can begin to help out as well. And don't forget about the school counselor as a resource. Sometimes students are afraid to open up to their teachers because they are with them every day, but they often will share with a counselor who has a private office that they can visit when they need someone to listen.

CHAPTER 3

Although most professionals don't want to believe that fellow teachers can act this selfishly, circumstances such as these will more than likely occur at some point in your experience in education. For a variety of reasons, some educators want to control their "territory"; unfortunately, this can include the young people that they work with. First, don't become angry or frustrated by this problem; instead, identify it and devise a plan to improve your own professional skills. Second, since you have discovered an area where you need improvement, seek out other coworkers who will be more helpful.

Remember that there are specialists on campus who have training in how to meet the needs of special students. This might also be a time for you to pick up a book or take another class to increase your knowledge and skills in this area. Finally, don't be afraid to ask for assistance, and certainly don't get sidetracked by one person who isn't helping you grow as a person or professional.

CHAPTER 4

While Jessica has obvious interpersonal strengths, somehow others appear to misunderstand her, perhaps because they aren't as gifted in this area. You may want to reassure Jessica that you appreciate her communication and relational abilities and offer her several examples of how she has added something positive to the profession. Be sure not to talk unprofessionally about other colleagues, but provide Jessica with some possible reasons why they might be responding the way they are.

In order to help Jessica become more sensitive to the strengths and weaknesses of her coworkers, you might recommend that she try toning down her enthusiasm at least for a while. She could listen more to other staff members and ask them questions about what they like or think about various subjects. Meanwhile, Jessica's fellow professionals may end up missing her interactions with them, and they might actually make some attempts to reach out to her, too.

CHAPTER 5

Although most educators hope that there will never be scenarios like this on school campuses, sadly, there are bound to be occasional problems of this sort. Be sure that you remind Bob of this as a means of providing a simple reality check. You might share a story about your own dealings with conflict in job settings. In addition, you might suggest that Bob ask himself whether or not he truly enjoys working on the extra projects and committees. If he does, then that is reason enough for him to continue what he's doing.

Also, Bob can be reassured that these outside efforts benefit both the students and the school. It might cause some problems for Bob if he addresses these concerns with his principal, but by doing so he will create more opportunities for open dialogue. He may also have the chance to make suggestions about how to get all of the staff more involved in these types of activities. Above all, encourage Bob to remain professional, even with these coworkers who are putting pressure on him.

CHAPTER 6

There are many interpersonal dynamics at work in this conundrum, so it's essential to take time to reflect on situations such as these well before they arise in your teaching experience. For example, the caregivers in this scenario are more-or-less burned out when it comes to parenting as well as their involvement with schools. Then there is a child who is struggling and disinterested in school.

As an educator, you must address the needs of the child and provide the parents with helpful hints without overstepping your boundaries as a classroom teacher. In other words, you are not Gabriella's third parent! As tired as these caregivers are, ultimately she is their responsibility; they must become the expert on their child. A gentle reminder of this should be the first step toward solving the problem at hand. For example, you could begin your conversation with a statement such as, "I realize it must be very difficult raising four children today, but Gabriella still appreciates all of the interest you are showing her. Your involvement in her life will really make a difference in how she does at school this year and in the years to come."

Once this is out of the way, you can provide more specific tips on how to meet her needs in math, including some thoughts about rewarding Gabriella for improvement. Finally, you can point out that, although athletics are important, this should be an area to include in Gabriella's incentive program for bringing up her academic grades. In other words, they could let her know that unless her math grade rises, she will have to temporarily leave the softball team. Your main focus should be to let the parents know you are concerned and are working toward assisting their child, but you cannot help Gabriella alone.

CHAPTER 7

In a situation such as this, the individual's relationship style (or lack thereof) has put you in an uncomfortable position. When this happens, it's normal for frustration levels to rise. The most appropriate step to take at this point is to get additional feedback from someone you trust. Ask a colleague about this person—for example, does she normally treat staff members this way? Perhaps your coworker will have some other insights about how to approach her. Be sure to ask if anyone has tried to do further intervention; in other words, has an administrator ever been apprised of the situation? What was done? Were those steps successful?

After this discussion, if you still feel that you need assistance with this problem, then set up an appointment with your administrator. Be sure to write down some of the incidents that have occurred (keeping documentation of recurring work-related problems is always beneficial) and share them at this meeting.

Although not every situation will have a happy ending, most of them will improve. Sometimes the individual in question is having personal problems of his or her own that are interfering with job performance. If so, then you may be the first one to guide this person toward an intervention that will lead to some sort of resolution.

CHAPTER 8

Like many students that you will encounter, Kevin is a perfect example of a young person who is inexperienced when it comes to the "other." In this case, the "others" are the ELL students, but later on it could be a particular racial group, a child with a disability, or simply someone who he perceives as being different than himself. Therefore, Kevin should have an opportunity to experience real life in the small world that is your classroom.

The best place to start is to immediately talk to Kevin about his need to work with his fellow classmates. Remind him that you are all on the same team and must learn to get along. Second, assure him that you will be stopping by throughout the project to check on him and his group. In many instances students simply react strangely to new situations because they are unsure about how they will do without some support. Finally, let Kevin know that if he has any other concerns, he should always feel free to come and share them with you.

In your role as facilitator, be certain that you make regular rounds in the classroom as the students are working. This will be of benefit to all students, but particularly to this group, which you already have a good idea may need some extra guidance. As you pause at Kevin's table, look at how the students are interacting, and be sure to praise them for positive communication, teamwork, and rapport building. For example, "Dahlia, I really like the way that you shared your colored pens with Kevin. And Kevin, your polite thank you to Dahlia shows her that you appreciate her efforts. Good job, Table Four!"

CHAPTER 9

Unfortunately, you will discover that there are many people like Ms. McKnight in this profession: dedicated and driven, but lacking the personal balance needed to experience the real joy of teaching. Although you may not be able to change her perspective about what it takes to be an exceptional educator, you must certainly stand up for what is best for you. Scheduling a meeting with her sooner rather than later is critical (and since she likes to meet, this shouldn't present a problem).

During this conversation, discuss the reasons why *you* need to exercise, eat lunch with your coworkers, and have other activities in your life that keep you happy, healthy, and well-balanced. In other words, don't make it about her—simply share *your* needs. This is also the perfect opportunity to set some personal boundaries with her; let Kathy know what days you're willing to stay late, and discuss the items that she feels are most vital during those times. Once you've established these boundaries, be sure to stick to them. Who knows, maybe your attempts at a more balanced life will get her thinking about making healthy adjustments as well.

Seven Steps to Plug All Students into Learning

1. Make sure all kids feel connected to you, one another, and what is going on in your classroom.
2. Provide a curriculum that the students can relate to; if yours is lacking in this area, add content that is meaningful whenever and wherever you can!
3. Look for multicultural materials to enhance your content areas as well as opportunities to combine cultural activities with your curriculum.
4. Be sure your instruction is active, not passive! Get your students involved in the learning process.
5. Learn how to be a facilitator. While you should still be in charge of the class, give your students opportunities to work together as much as possible.
6. Think outside the box! Just because things have been done at your school a certain way, doesn't mean that they can't (or shouldn't) change!
7. "What the world needs now is love. . . ." Don't forget that a little TLC (tender loving care) will go a lot farther than a whole lot of uncompassionate discipline.

"Have You Seen Stephanie?"

Jim Wickstrom

It was a hot day in late August, and the temperature was well into the 80s by 10:00 A.M. I had just unloaded several boxes from my cabinets in preparation for the new school year beginning the next week. My bulletin boards were only half up and as I searched for more T-pins I could feel the beads of sweat on my forehead, even though I was wearing a T-shirt and shorts.

A girl suddenly appeared at the door and with a big smile excitedly asked when school was starting. As I glanced over my shoulder and said, "Next week," I suddenly realized that this girl was ready for school right now! She had her backpack on and was dressed as if she had come out of the '60s. Her black velvet dress was trimmed with lace, and her patent leather shoes seemed strikingly out of place for such a hot day, school or no school.

"Would you like to help?" I asked. She nodded and proceeded to help with the bulletin boards and name tags. As we worked, I noticed that her dress appeared to be quite old and was worn in several places. (I found out later that the dress had belonged to her mother.) It certainly wasn't the typical sixth-grade middle school outfit. Her name was Stephanie, and she lived in a small apartment across the street from the school, in Escondido, with her mother and seventh-grader brother. She said her brother was out playing and her mother wasn't home.

Monday morning brought a gaggle of children to my door all dressed in their new school clothes, holding backpacks, lunches, and big smiles on their faces. Stephanie was there, too, wearing the same black velvet dress with patent leather shoes and frilly socks. Several of the boys wearing the cool Quicksilver shirts and shorts snickered at her choice of clothing, but she seemed unaffected by their rudeness.

The first day of school went well. Children socialized well together inside and outside of the classroom. All except Stephanie. She was never included in any group and was always by herself. When the bell rang for the kids to go home, everyone rushed out the door. I noticed that Stephanie, though, was still hard at work at her desk.

"Don't you have to get home, Stephanie?" I asked.

"No," she said matter-of-factly.

"Isn't someone waiting for you?"

"No, but my brother might be home around six," she explained while still writing.

"When will your mom get home?" I asked.

"I don't know because she is in the hospital."

"How long has she been there?" I asked.

"Three weeks, this time."

"Who takes care of you when she isn't home?" I wondered out loud.

"My mother's friend," she said while getting out her math homework.

With a little more research, I discovered that Stephanie's mother was an acute diabetic and had been in and out of the hospital for the past year. Because of her weight and drug abuse she was not able to control her blood sugar level by herself and constantly depended on the hospital staff. Her current stay was approaching one month, and she was having trouble cashing the welfare checks from her hospital bed.

The children's designated caretaker was a male biker who lived across town and stopped by every day or two to make sure Stephanie and her brother had enough food and supplies. I later discovered that some weeks he would only stop by once or twice, and if it wasn't for the free breakfasts and lunches at school the kids would never have enough food. He neglected to tell me that the phone bill hadn't been paid in two months.

In the first three weeks of school, I had seen Stephanie wear only three different sets of clothes and, after visiting her mother in the hospital, I decided to make a home visit. Our walk home after school provided me with quite an education. At first sight, the apartment Stephanie lived in was cluttered with overflowing trashcans, piles of old clothes on the floor, one worn-out couch, and a small TV. The beds contained a well-worn bottom sheet and a torn and stained blanket on top. It became painfully obvious that these two children were living on their own!

As I drove home that night, I decided to take action. I called the local Mervyns Clothing Store and convinced the manager to donate $200 worth of clothing. After school the next day Stephanie, her brother, and I went on a shopping spree! Although both kids walked away thrilled, I was shocked to find out how much $200 doesn't buy. Two classroom parent volunteers joined me in finding used clothing from their church and friends in the children's sizes. They were awesome! Even Stephanie's classmates quietly got involved and were supportive. One parent went to Stephanie's apartment to help clean up, wash clothes, and organize closets. Her report back to me was troubling.

The only food in the house was two old boxes of macaroni and cheese, a large container of powdered fruit drink, and one pop tart! The only food and nutrition the children were getting was at school! No one knew where the supposed food money was going.

Again, the parent volunteers went into action, collecting cereal, milk, bread, peanut butter, vegetables, fruit, and other basics for the apartment. Our parent "team" rotated visits to make sure they were fed and well.

During the next three months, Stephanie's mother was home a total of two weeks, yet Stephanie never missed a day of school. Our parent conference took place at her hospital bed. Now, however, I was the one having difficulty emotionally. I was being torn in two trying to decide whether to call Child Protective Services (CPS) on the issue of neglect, as California law requires. Stephanie's mother's health was now deteriorating with a heart problem, and she pleaded with me not to report her to CPS. A friend of the family confided that Stephanie's mother "might not make it" if her children were taken away.

Even though we had provided a safe, nurturing environment for Stephanie at school, her life as we knew it was hanging by a thread. On a Tuesday in late January Stephanie didn't show up for school. Her phone had been disconnected. When I called the apartment manager to see if he could go check on the children, his comments to me said it all. Stephanie and her brother were being evicted because of overdue rent payments.

The landlord needed $550 now or they were locking them out of the apartment! Frantically, I looked for a solution. During my break I called Emmanuel Faith Church because I knew they were active in the community, and I asked to talk with the minister. The church secretary told me that he wasn't available but said I could talk with the youth minister. As he came on the phone my voice started to break. Gathering all of the composure I could, I blurted out, "You don't know me but I'm a teacher at Grant School and one of my student's mother is in the hospital and they are being evicted. I need $550 right now." All he said was, "I think I can help you."

At 11:15 A.M. my school office called and said that a man was coming down to my classroom to see me. While my students worked diligently on their social studies assignment, a man in his early thirties walked in and handed me a plain white envelope. It contained five $100 bills, two twenties, and a ten. I wanted to say thank you, but nothing came out. I just struggled to compose myself.

At lunch I called the apartment manager and arranged for the payment. He said that this would be fine for now, but he would require future rent payments in advance. Stephanie's mother hadn't been paying the rent, and we had only achieved a one-month reprieve! As the month went on, I discovered that it wouldn't matter.

Stephanie's thirty-one-year-old mother died of heart failure. The hospital called the next of kin, Stephanie's aunt, who lived in Colorado. It took her two days to make the funeral arrangements, sift through the house for important documents, and obtain temporary custody of the children.

After the funeral I met with Stephanie's aunt. She appeared drained and haggard and was desperate to be briefed on Stephanie and her brother. When we were finished she said, "Thank you! You have told me more about Stephanie and her brother in 30 minutes than anyone has for the last three days!" She said that she would be taking the children to Colorado that night to live with her family.

Later I stopped by the apartment to say good-bye, but I had just missed them. I saw that the door was unlocked, and when I peeked inside I noticed that nothing had changed. There were still overflowing trash cans, piles of old clothes on the floor, and dirty plates in the sink. Then, over in the corner on the floor I saw the worn-out, black velvet dress with the lace on it. She had left it behind. Stephanie had closed one chapter in her life and had begun a new one. A month later I received a letter from Stephanie thanking me for all I had done. She said she liked her new school and friends in Colorado and was doing well.

You will meet Stephanie in your classroom someday, but she may not be easy to spot. She will be of no particular race or gender, and you may have to look for the subtleties in the classroom or make a home visit . . . or search into her eyes. Will you be able to recognize her? Or will your vision be clouded by the constant push to keep your students on task to learn all of the standards and pass the California CAT 6 tests or by the pressures of No Child Left Behind?

References

Armstrong, T. (1999). *7 Kinds of Smart: Identifying and Developing Your Multiple Intelligences*. New York: Plume.

Banks, J. A. (2001). *Cultural Diversity and Education: Foundations, Curriculum, and Teaching*, 4th ed. Boston: Allyn & Bacon.

Berliner, D. C., & Biddle, B. J. (1995). *The Manufactured Crisis: Myths, Fraud, and the Attack on America's Public Schools*. New York: Addison-Wesley.

Blanchard, K., Zigarmi, P., & Zigarmi, D. (1985). *Leadership and the One-Minute Manager: Increasing Effectiveness through Situational Leadership*. New York: Morrow.

Bloom, B. S. (1964). *Stability and Change in Human Characteristics*. New York: Wiley.

Boutte, G. S. (2002). *Resounding Voices: School Experiences of People from Diverse Ethnic Backgrounds*. Boston: Allyn & Bacon.

Burmark, L., & Fournier, L. (2003). *Enlighten Up! An Educator's Guide to Stress-Free Living*. Alexandria, VA: ASCD.

Children's Defense Fund. (1998). *The State of America's Children Yearbook*. Washington, DC: Children's Defense Fund.

Clark, B. (1979). *Growing Up Gifted*. Columbus: Merrill.

Cloud, H., & Townsend, J. (1992). *Boundaries: When to Say Yes, When to Say No, to Take Control of Your Life*. Grand Rapids, MI: Zondervan.

Cole, R. W. (Ed.). (1995). *Educating Everybody's Children: Diverse Teaching Strategies for Diverse Learners*. Alexandria, VA: ASCD.

Collins, J. (2001). *Good to Great: Why Some Companies Make the Leap and Others Don't*. New York: HarperCollins.

Comer, J. P., Ben-Avie, M., Haynes, N. M., & Joyner, E. T., Eds. (1999). *Child by Child: The Comer Process for Change in Education*. New York: Teachers College Press.

Comer, J. P., Haynes, N. M., Joyner, E. T., & Ben-Avie, M. (1996). *Rallying the Whole Village: The Comer Process for Reforming Education*. New York: Teachers College Press.

Cushner, K. (1999). *Human Diversity in Action: Developing Multicultural Competencies for the Classroom*. Boston: McGraw-Hill College.

Darling-Hammond, L. (1997). *The Right to Learn: A Blueprint for Creating Schools That Work*. San Francisco: Jossey-Bass.

Darling-Hammond, L., Wise, A. E., & Klein, S. P. (1999). *A License to Teach: Raising Standards for Teaching*. San Francisco: Jossey-Bass.

Deal, T. E., & Kennedy, A. A. (1982). *Corporate Cultures*. Reading, MA: Addison-Wesley.

DeRoche, E. F., & Williams, M. M. (2001). *Educating Hearts and Minds: A Comprehensive Character Education Framework*. Thousand Oaks, CA: Corwin.

Dewey, J. (1933). *How We Think*. Lexington, MA: Heath.

Doty, G. (2001). *Fostering Emotional Intelligence in K–8 Students*. Thousand Oaks, CA: Corwin.

Fiore, T. A., & Curtin, T. R. (1997). *Public and Private School Principals in the United States: A Statistical Profile, 1987–88 to 1993–94*. Washington, DC: U.S. Department of Education, Office of Educational Research and Improvement.

Fix, M., & Passel, J. S. (1994). Immigrants and social services. *Migration World 22* (4), 22–25.

Freeman, Y. S., & Freeman, D. E. (1998). *ESL/EFT Teaching: Principles for Success*. Portsmouth, NH: Heinemann.

Fullan, M. (1994). *Change Forces: Probing the Depths of Educational Reform*. London: Flamer.

Fullan, M. (2001). *Leading in a Culture of Change*. San Francisco: Jossey-Bass.

Gabelnick, F., MacGregor, J., Matthews, R. S., & Smith, B. L. (1990). *Learning Communities: Creating Connections among Students, Faculty, and Disciplines*. San Francisco: Jossey-Bass.

Garcia, E. (2002). *Student Cultural Diversity: Understanding and Meeting the Challenge*, 3rd ed. Boston: Houghton Mifflin.

Gardner, H. (1983). *Frames of Mind: The Theory of Multiple Intelligences*. New York: Basic.

Gardner, H. (1999). *Intelligence Reframed: Multiple Intelligences for the 21st Century*. New York: Basic.

Goleman, D. (1995). *Emotional Intelligence: Why It Can Matter More Than IQ*. New York: Bantam.

Goleman, D., Boyatzis, R., & McKee, A. (2002). *Primal Leadership: Realizing the Power of Emotional Intelligence.* Boston: Harvard Business School Press.

Gordon, H., & Gordon, R. (Trans.). (1951). *The Education of Man.* New York: Philosophical Library.

Gordon, S. P. (1994). *How to Help Beginning Teachers Succeed.* Alexandria, VA: Association for Supervision and Curriculum Development.

Greider, W. (1997). *One World: Ready or Not.* New York: Simon & Schuster.

Grissmer, D. W., Kirby, S. N., Berends, M., & Williamson, S. (1994). *Student Achievement and the Changing American Family.* Santa Monica, CA: RAND.

Henze, R., Katz, A., Norte, E., Sather, S. E., & Walker, E. (2002). *Leading for Diversity: How School Leaders Promote Positive Interethnic Relations.* Thousand Oaks, CA: Corwin.

Howard, G. R. (1999). *We Can't Teach What We Don't Know: White Teachers, Multiracial Schools.* New York: Teachers College Press.

Jensen, R. A., & Kiley, T. J. (2000). *Teaching, Leading, and Learning: Becoming Caring Professionals.* Boston: Houghton Mifflin.

Jenson, R. (1998). *Taking the Lead: Following the Example of Paul, Timothy, & Silvanus.* Sisters, OR: Multnomah.

Johnson, D. W., Johnson, R. T., & Holubec, E. J. (1994). *Cooperative Learning in the Classroom.* Alexandria, VA: ASCD.

Joyce, B., & Weil, M. (1996). *Models of Teaching,* 5th ed. Boston: Allyn & Bacon.

Kaluger, G., & Kaluger, M. F. (1979). *Human Development: The Span of Life,* 2nd ed. St. Louis: Mosby.

Keefe, J. W., & Jenkins, J. M. (1997). *Instruction and the Learning Environment.* Larchmont, NY: Eye on Education.

Kincheloe, J. L. (2004). The knowledges of teacher education: developing a critical complex epistemology. *Teacher Education Quarterly, 31* (1), 49–66.

Krashen, S. (1981). *Second Language Acquisition and Second Language Learning.* New York: Pergamon.

Lencioni, P. (2002). *The Five Dysfunctions of a Team: A Leadership Fable.* San Francisco: Jossey-Bass.

Lindberg, J. A., & Swick, A. M. (2002). *Common-Sense Classroom Management: Surviving September and Beyond in the Elementary Classroom.* Thousand Oaks, CA: Corwin.

Mendler, A. N. (2001). *Connecting with Children.* Alexandria, VA: ASCD.

Micklethwait, J., & Woolbridge, A. (2000). *A Future Perfect: The Challenge and Hidden Promise of Globalization.* New York: Random House.

Moecker, D. L. (November 1992). Special education decision process: for Anglo and Hispanic students. Paper presented at the Council for Exceptional Children Topical Conference on Culturally and Linguistically Diverse Exceptional Children, Minneapolis.

National Education Association. (2004). *Education Support Professionals.* Available at www.nea.org/esphome/.

National Society for the Study of Education. (1979). *The Gifted and Talented: Their Education and Development.* Chicago: University of Chicago Press.

Nieto, S. (2000). *Affirming Diversity: The Sociopolitical Context of Multicultural Education,* 3rd ed. New York: Longman.

Nobscot Corporation, Retention Management and Metrics (2002). Available at www.nobscot.com/about /teacher_retention_strategies.cfm.

Nordgren, R. D. (2002). Globalization and education: what students will need to know and be able to do in the global village. *Phi Delta Kappan, 84* (4), 318–321.

Odden, A. R. (1995). *Educational Leadership for America's Schools.* New York: McGraw-Hill.

Orange, C. (2002). *The Quick Reference Guide to Educational Innovations: Practices, Programs, Policies, and Philosophies.* Thousand Oaks, CA: Corwin.

Ornstein, A. C., & Levine, D. U. (2000). *Foundations of Education,* 7th ed. Boston: Houghton Mifflin.

Ovando, C., & McLaren, P., Eds. (2000). *The Politics of Multiculturalism and Bilingual Education: Students and Teachers Caught in the Cross Fire.* Boston: McGraw-Hill.

Partin, R. L. (1999). *Classroom Teachers Survival Guide: Practical Strategies, Management Techniques, and Reproducibles for New and Experienced Teachers.* West Nyack, NY: Center for Applied Research in Education.

Rasinski, T. V. (1995). *Parents and Teachers Helping Children Learn to Read and Write.* Fort Worth, TX: Harcourt Brace College.

Santrock, J. W. (1983). *Life-Span Development.* Dubuque, IA: William C. Brown.

Schaps, E. (2003). Creating a school community. *Educational Leadership, 60* (6), 31–33.

Shea, T. M., & Bauer, A. M. (1997). *An Introduction to Special Education: A Social Systems Perspective,* 2nd ed. Chicago: Brown & Benchmark.

Smith, T. E. C., Polloway, E. A., Patton, J. R., & Dowdy, C. A. (2001). *Teaching Students with Special Needs in Inclusive Settings,* 3rd ed. Boston: Allyn and Bacon.

Snyder, K. J., Acker-Hocevar, M., & Snyder, K. M. (1999). *Living on the Edge of Chaos: Leading Schools into the Global Age.* Milwaukee: American Society for Quality.

Sornson, R., & Scott, J. (1997). *Teaching and Joy*. Alexandria, VA: ASCD.

Sprenger, M. (2002). *Becoming a "Wiz" at Brain-Based Teaching: How to Make Every Year Your Best Year*. Thousand Oaks, CA: Corwin.

Spring, J. (2002). *American Education*, 10th ed. Boston: McGraw-Hill.

Stanford University. (2000). *The San Diego City Schools Reform Initiative: Views from the Inside*. Palo Alto, CA: Center for the Study of Teaching and Policy, Stanford University.

Sweeny, B. (1990). The new teacher mentoring process: A working model. *Teachermentor.com*. Available at www.teachermentor.com/Mentorsite/MentoringProcess.html.

Takaki, R. (1993). *A Different Mirror: A History of Multicultural America*. Boston: Little, Brown and Company.

Tiedt, P. L., & Tiedt, I. M. (1999). *Multicultural Teaching: A Handbook of Activities, Information, and Resources*, 5th ed. Boston: Allyn & Bacon.

Toffler, A., & Toffler, H. (1995). *Creating a New Civilization: The Politics of the Third Wave*. Atlanta: Turner.

U.S. Bureau of the Census. (1992). *Marital Status and Living Arrangements: March, 1992*. Current Population Reports, Series P20, No. 468. Washington, DC: U.S. Department of Commerce.

U.S. Department of Education. (1996). *Introducing Goals 2000: A World-Class Education for Every Child*. Washington, DC: U.S. Department of Education.

Vance, P. S. (1991). The initiating-extended-role teacher: exploring facets of teacher leadership. *Dissertation Abstracts International, 53*, 01A-60.

Weah, W., Simmons, V. C., & Hall, M. (2000). Service-learning and multicultural/multiethnic perspectives: from diversity to equity. *Annual Editions Multicultural Education, 2001/2002*, 186–189.

Weil, A. (1997). *8 Weeks to Optimum Health: A Proven Program for Taking Full Advantage of Your Body's Natural Healing Power*. New York: Ballantine Books.

Weinstein, C. S. (1996). *Secondary Classroom Management*. Boston: McGraw-Hill.

Wilke, R. L. (2003). *The First Days of Class: A Practical Guide for the Beginning Teacher*. Thousand Oaks, CA: Corwin.

Witty, P. (1940). Some considerations in the education of gifted children. *Educational Administration and Supervision, 26*, 512–521.

Wong, H. K., & Wong, R. T. (1998). *The First Day of School: How to Be an Effective Teacher*, 2nd ed. Mountain View, CA: Wong.

Zachary, L. J. (2000). *The Mentor's Guide: Facilitating Effective Learning Relationships*. San Francisco: Jossey-Bass.

Additional Resources

Armstrong, T. (1994). *Multiple Intelligences in the Classroom*. Alexandria, VA: ASCD.

Armstrong, T. (1998). *Awakening Genius in the Classroom*. Alexandria, VA: ASCD.

Armstrong, T. (1999). *7 Kinds of Smart: Identifying and Developing Your Multiple Intelligences*. New York: Penguin Putnam.

Campbell, L., Campbell, B., & Dickinson, D. (1998). *Teaching and Learning through Multiple Intelligences*, 2nd ed. Boston: Pearson, Allyn & Bacon.

Gardner, H. (1993). *Frames of Mind: The Theory of Multiple Intelligences 10th Anniversary Edition*. New York: Basic.

Gardner, H. (1993). *Multiple Intelligences: The Theory in Practice, A Reader*. New York: Basic.

Gardner, H. (1999). *Intelligence Reframed: Multiple Intelligences for the 21st Century*. New York: Basic.

Kornhaber, M., Fierros, E., & Veenema, S. (2003). *Multiple Intelligences: Best Ideas from Research and Practice*. Boston: Pearson, Allyn & Bacon.

Nielson, K. (1999). *Developing Students' Multiple Intelligences (Grades K–8)*. New York: Scholastic.

Teacher Created Materials, Inc. (1999). *The Best of Multiple Intelligences Activities*. Westminster, CA: Teacher Created Materials.

Index

About the Author

Rebecca Lynn Wilke, Ed.D., is a university professor and educational and leadership consultant. Dr. Wilke has worked with children and adults of all ages in public and private school settings for over twenty years. In addition, she and her husband, Dr. Steve Wilke, operate LEADon, Inc., an organization dedicated to transforming the personal and professional lives of corporate leaders across America. They provide preemployment assessment, executive coaching, high-performance team building, group training, and leadership evaluations for everyone, from interns to executives. Dr. Wilke is a graduate of the University of Southern California, where she specialized in educational leadership and multicultural education. She can be reached on the World Wide Web at Leadon.biz or via e-mail at doctorswilke@cox.net.